MARIA TERMINI is deeply involved in silkscreening as a working and exhibiting artist and as a teacher in the Boston area. She has had several exhibits of her prints and has executed many mural commissions that can be seen in the Boston area.

THE ART AND DESIGN SERIES

For beginners, students, and working professionals
in both fine and commercial arts, these books offer
practical, how-to introductions to a variety of areas
in contemporary art and design.

Each illustrated volume is written by a working artist,
a specialist in his or her field, and each concentrates
on an individual area—from advertising layout or
printmaking to interior design, painting, and
cartooning, among others. Each contains information
artists will find useful in the studio, in the classroom,
and in the marketplace.

SILKSCREENING

maria
termini

A SPECTRUM BOOK

PRENTICE-HALL, INC., Englewood Cliffs, New Jersey 07632

Library of Congress Cataloging in Publication Data

TERMINI, MARIA.
　Silkscreening.

　(The Art & design series) (A Spectrum Book)
　Includes index.
　1. Screen process printing.　I. Title.
TT273.T47　　764′.8　　77-10719
ISBN 0-13-809996-0
ISBN 0-13-809988-X pbk.

A Spectrum Book

10　9　8　7　6　5　4　3　2　1

Printed in the United States of America

PRENTICE-HALL INTERNATIONAL, INC., London
PRENTICE-HALL OF AUSTRALIA PTY. LIMITED, Sydney
PRENTICE-HALL OF CANADA, LTD., Toronto
PRENTICE-HALL OF INDIA PRIVATE LIMITED, New Delhi
PRENTICE-HALL OF JAPAN, INC., Tokyo
PRENTICE-HALL OF SOUTHEAST ASIA PTE. LTD., Singapore
WHITEHALL BOOKS LIMITED, Wellington, New Zealand

**To my children, Tom and Warren,
and to the music of colors**

Special thanks to **Cynthia R. Benjamins** for all the black-and-white photos and to the following people for the photos of the color plates:

- Marja Lianko-Roberts for her "Parakeet Rhapsody No. 1"
- Bonita Barlow for her "Birth"
- Biron Valier for his "Silver Top Diner" and for Paula Latos-Valier's "A Little Dab'll Do Ya"
- Deac Rossell for Michaela Meyers' "The Wandering Eye" and "Wendy's Garden"
- Tim Hamill for his "Negative Foliage," "Modular Pholage," and "Paleontologist's Dream"
- Victoria Porras for her "Structure No. 4"

CONTENTS

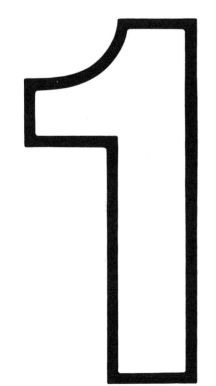

INTRODUCTION

Silkscreening is a new, exciting printmaking method with many advantages over other printing methods. It is basically uncomplicated and requires very little technical knowledge. The same screen can be used over and over again for many colors and stencils. It is quite easy to produce as many prints as you want with no deterioration in quality, and it is also possible to print on almost any kind of surface.

Silkscreen inks dry very fast, often within fifteen minutes, so it is possible to do multicolored prints in a few hours' time. The color on silkscreened prints is brilliant and intense because it is stenciled on, not stamped on as in relief printing.

You have great freedom and flexibility in preparing the screen. Unlike block printing, there is no need to reverse the image as the stencil is prepared. Lettering can be done exactly as it is to appear.

All kinds of visual effects are possible—from large, flat areas of rich color to delicate transparent shadings, from thin, precise lines to photographic images. A quick glance at the color plates in this book will illustrate the enormous variety of styles and expression that is possible.

Silkscreening is a stencil method without limitations. Working with stencils cut from heavy paper presents the problem of how to keep the inside parts of the stencil in position while maintaining freedom in designing. In silkscreening there is no such problem with loose floating parts because the silk holds all parts of the design in position.

In the silkscreen process the design is printed by squeezing ink through the open areas of a piece of silk that has been very tightly stretched on a wooden frame. The piece of silk has been blocked out with various stencil materials in those areas that are to be unprinted; the spaces to be printed are left open. This is the principle underlying the printing of all silkscreen images, whether they be on paper, fabric, or whatever: the open areas of the silk print (that is, they allow the ink to be squeezed through to the material underneath) and the closed areas block printing.

Figure 1.1 Silkscreening in action. Ink is being squeegeed through the open areas of a silkscreen to produce a print on the paper beneath it.

Figure 1.2 A print done from a torn paper stencil. The stencil on the screen serves to block out the silk in those areas to be left unprinted. The ink penetrates the open areas of the silk.

A stencil is produced on the silk to block out the screen as desired.

There are four main stencil methods: **paper, glue, hand-cut film,** and **photo-stencil film.** In each of these, the stencils may be removed from the screen, and so the screen can be used over and over again. A separate stencil may be used for each color, or new colors may be formed by overlapping transparent colors.

Silkscreening is a fascinating art that calls for manual and mental skill. The more you do it, the easier it becomes. What seems very awkward at first will, with practice, become more natural. Some aspects of the technique are very difficult to describe in words, for example, what is good squeegee pressure. However, with practice you will gain a sense of what works. There are even ways to be very fast and organized about the messy part—cleaning up.

I have written this book to explain the mechanics of silkscreening, to help the beginner know what supplies are needed, how to set up a work place efficiently, and how to establish a layout and register a print.

There are separate chapters for each stencil method, presented in their order of difficulty. It would be wise to start off in silkscreening by using paper stencils, which are quick and inexpensive, before moving on to other more complex and time-consuming methods.

I have included many illustrations, from my own work and from that of other Boston area printmakers, chosen as good examples of certain stencil methods. Each stencil method has its own visual characteristics. The photographic illustrations clearly demonstrate the important steps in the various methods by showing experienced hands in action.

There are things you can do on your own to enhance your knowledge. Looking at silkscreen prints in galleries and museums can be enjoyable and helpful. Silkscreen courses offered in most adult education programs and art schools can be worthwhile, and working with an experienced teacher can really accelerate your progress. You can also learn a lot from seeing what other people are doing.

Try to read the chapters thoroughly before you start. Be sure you have all the necessary materials on hand, have a good supply of rags handy, wear old clothes—and **relax!**

Don't worry about being creative. Just be yourself. Feel free to experiment with colors and shapes. Don't expect everything always to come out as it was planned. Surprises can be just as interesting.

As a teacher, I have been aware of some very specific problem areas and of questions that students ask most frequently. I have tried to clarify these areas of confusion, hoping to simplify things and lessen frustration.

As an artist, I hope that I can pass on to you some of the knowledge I have gained working and experimenting in my studio.

In short, I have tried to take the mystery out of silkscreening. But remember, there is always lots of room for the magic.

HOW SILK SCREENING DEVELOPED

2

Silkscreening is a relatively new printing method, developed during this century as a commercial art method to replace time-consuming stenciling and hand lettering. It is only within the last forty years that it has been used as a way of producing fine-arts prints.

Stenciling is a very old art form. There is evidence that suggests that prehistoric cave paintings were done using STENCILS* cut from large leaves to repeat design elements. Stenciling has been used extensively in the folk art of many nations for decorating walls, fabrics, and furniture. In simple stenciling the image is produced by rubbing ink through the open areas of the stencil material. However, the craftspeople who did stenciling always had to reckon with one big limitation: if there were spaces within the design that were to remain uncolored, there had to be a way to hold these "island" parts in position attached to the main part of the stencil.

Thin connecting bridges of stencil material were most often used to hold these parts in place. This often interfered with the smooth flow of a design and restricted stenciling to very simple shapes. It was the Japanese who attempted to solve this problem of loose floating shapes by using strands of silk to hold the pieces in position.

* Words that are set in SMALL CAPITALS within the text are defined in the Glossary.

Figure 2.1 A lettering stencil of thick paper sold in stationery stores. Notice how bridges of stencil paper are holding the parts of the stencil together.

Around 1900, American commercial artists started using a wooden frame stretched tightly with silk, and the art of silkscreening was born. The loose FLOATING PARTS could be attached to the silk or formed on the silk itself. Now that there was no longer a need for connecting bridges, stenciling gained a new kind of freedom. The time-consuming stencil brush was replaced by the SQUEEGEE, a strip of rubber in a wooden handle. The squeegee could quickly spread the ink evenly through the open areas of the silk to print a clean design.

Silkscreening was used exclusively as a commercial process until the late 1930s, when artists began to explore the technique as a printmaking medium. Government grants from the Works Projects Administration provided artists both time and materials with which to work and experiment, and soon the first public exhibition of silkscreen prints was held. These early silkscreen artists—among them Guy Maccoy, Robert Gwathmy, Elizabeth Olds, and Philip Hicken—produced prints that often had the character of a watercolor: thin, wash-like areas of color with brushed shapes. These artists were primarily painters—pioneers working in a new, unknown medium—and their natural impulse was to imitate something with which they were already quite familiar.

Through these exhibits, the public became more aware of this new printmaking process. The art critic Carl Zirgosser coined the term **serigraph,** derived from the Greek language, to distinguish a silkscreen fine-arts print that eventually would be framed and hung on a wall from one that had a specific commercial function. **Serigraph** literally means printed through silk, just as the word **lithograph** (also from the Greek) means printed through stone. The term SERIGRAPHY refers to the process of printing a serigraph. For the sake of consistency, I will use the word **silkscreening.**

Artists continued working in silkscreen through the 1950s. It was about this time that silkscreen came into its own as a medium with unique and exciting characteristics. There were two good reasons for this.

First of all, important technical developments had taken place. Rich, well-formulated inks were now readily available and bright, intense colors could be produced. Also, the development of easy-to-use film stencils facilitated the entire process and ensured good results and clean prints.

Secondly, in the early 1960s certain art trends developed that were compatible with the silkscreen technique. Pop, Op (Optical) art, and Minimal art all displayed a clean, print-like style that was well served by silkscreening. Pop art reproduced, with certain kinds of emphasis, familiar commercial images that had first appeared in the print medium, such as Campbell Soup cans and Brillo boxes. Optical art explored the eye-dazzling possibilities of clean-edged geometric shapes, dots, and lines. Op art easily utilized the crisp knife-cut edges made possible by film stencils. Minimal art, a form that is sparse and geometric, required large, flat areas of color, free from the interference of brush strokes. All of these trends found dramatic expression in silkscreen prints, and the medium has been popularized through the work of such artists as Richard Anuszkiewicz, Corita Kent, Carol Summers, and Victor Vasarely.

Today, at a time when contemporary painting seems to have outdone itself, silkscreening is becoming especially relevant and is generating a lot of attention and interest. Paintings are too big and too expensive. Most big contemporary paintings wind up in offices, lobbies, or museums. There is a great need for smaller, more personal works of art for homes. Prints can fulfill this need, and more and more silkscreen prints are brightening up dull walls. They are not as expensive as paintings and are easy to store. A collection of prints can be changed as one wishes to give some interest and variety to any environment.

Silkscreening has many other uses in addition to its suitability as a fine-arts medium. Posters, greeting cards, wallpaper, wrapping paper, fabrics, bumper stickers, labels, ceramic tiles, and electronic circuits can all be printed with this same process. Although I have concentrated mainly on printing on paper, this being the most readily available and cheapest material to work with, the same stencil methods work on other surfaces as long as the right inks are used. There are special inks available for printing fabric, glass, plastic, metal, and so on. Most silkscreen suppliers publish free

Figure 2.2 A silkscreened poster.

catalogs that list the different kinds of silkscreen inks they stock and the special characteristics of these inks. For example, if color fastness is desired on silkscreened fabric, then special inks should be used, and the fabric should be heat-set for greater permanency (see Chapter 13 for a more-detailed explanation). For printing on plastics, there are special inks that adhere best to the plastic. Ceramic tiles can be printed using a glaze-like ink that is fired in the kiln and bonded to the tile. It is even possible to print the curved surface of a bottle by using a curved screen and squeegee.

The potential and uses of silkscreen are endless.

VISUAL EFFECTS OF SILKSCREENING

You can achieve almost any visual effect in silkscreening. The chart in Appendix A lists the four main stencil methods and the particular visual effects they produce. It is important to realize that each method has its own characteristics. Taking this into consideration when deciding which stencil method to use will save you a lot of time and frustration.

For example, if the design to be printed has large, flat shapes with clean edges, the most expedient way to reproduce it would be to use a tracing-paper stencil. If glue were used, it would have to dry before the printing could be done, and the edges of the shapes would not be as clean as they would had they been cut by a knife. On the other hand, if a design is more like a painting and the mark of the brush is an important part of the total effect, then the glue method would be most appropriate—either by itself or by first using a resist. If you want lettering that has very thin lines, the photo-stencil method would be the simplest to use. If the letters are to be thick and no smaller than approximately $\frac{3}{4}''$, then the glue method could be used.

The more you experiment with the different stencil methods, the more you will become aware of just which methods are best for specific projects. Looking at the prints in this book will help you become familiar with the effects of the different stencil methods. The captions will explain the methods that were used to create the prints.

Figure 3.1 Cut paper stencils.

Figure 3.2 This print was done using torn paper stencils and overlapping transparent colors.

Figure 3.3 Glue stencils, the top one done with tusche resist, the bottom using the glue alone.

Figure 3.4 Hand-cut film.

Figure 3.5 Photo stencils produced from flat, found-object positives: string, lace, and grass.

EQUIPMENT AND SUPPLIES

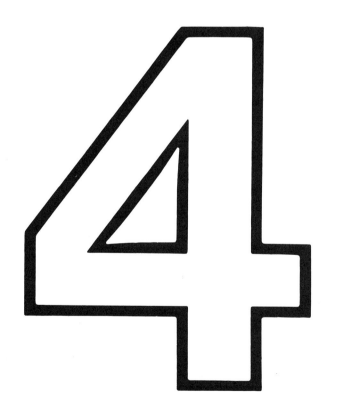

What follows is a complete list of basic materials needed to silkscreen using any of the four main stencil methods. More-detailed information follows in Chapters 5, 6, and 7. Some of the items, such as ink, silk, and films, will have to be purchased in an art store that sells silkscreen supplies. Other supplies can be bought in most art supply stores. Paint thinner and brush cleaner are cheaper in hardware stores. Most camera stores sell photo-flood bulbs. For your convenience, I have also listed the names and addresses of some of the larger manufacturers of silkscreen products in Appendix B. Check out local stores by phone and use the yellow pages. If you

Figure 4.1 Some suggested supplies for silkscreening.

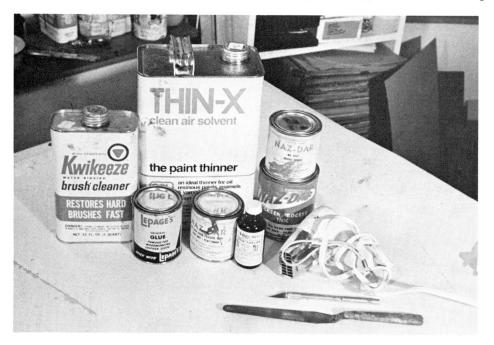

cannot get your supplies through a local store, write to the manufacturer and request the names of any stores in your area with whom you can do business by mail. If you write to these stores for information, you should ask them to send you a catalog of their products and prices. But before you start, read the list thoroughly. You may already have some of these things around your house.

- A screen approximately 12″ by 12″, stretched with size 12 mesh silk, attached to a baseboard with removable pin hinges
- A hard rubber squeegee to fit the screen; it should be $\frac{1}{2}$″ smaller than the inside width of the screen
- Oil-base poster inks specially formulated for silkscreening, an assortment of small cans of color
- Small tubes of oil color (these can replace ink when mixed with transparent base)
- Transparent base for mixing the ink to a good consistency
- Paint thinner
- Brush cleaner—the type sold in hardware stores, not the detergent type
- Tracing paper
- An X-acto knife with a no. 11 blade
- A package of refills for the knife
- Lepage's glue
- Tusche
- Stick tusche or crayons

- Masking tape, a $\frac{1}{2}''$ roll
- Ulanocut green—a hand-cut stencil film
- Blue Poly or Hi Fi Green—a presensitized photo-stencil film
- A no. 2 photo-flood bulb
- A piece of clean glass a little bit larger than the size of the film being exposed
- Film developer (A and B powders), or a 10% hydrogen peroxide solution
- Paper to print on—almost any kind of paper is suitable: drawing paper, bond paper, cover stock, construction paper, etc.
- Brushes of assorted sizes
- Scissors
- Rags
- Old newspapers
- Jars with screw top lids
- Small squares of rigid cardboard
- A hair dryer

SCREENS AND SQUEEGEES

Screens and squeegees are the basic equipment of silkscreening, as important as a printing press in offset printing. Silkscreening is a relatively inexpensive process, and you can buy a screen and squeegee for a relatively small amount of money, generally under $20. If you have more time than money, however, you can easily make your own screen.

Figure 5.1 A screen with an appropriately sized squeegee.

You only need one screen to get going, since the ink and the stencil are removed and the same silk used over and over again. All of the larger prints I have done have been printed with the same screen. In this way, the EDITION is truly limited—once the stencil is removed, there is no way to print that exact same image again. So, be sure you print all the copies you want before you clean off the STENCIL.

The silkscreen printing frame is made of wood, and the silk is stretched very tightly over it. Then, the frame is taped around the edges with gummed paper tape which is then sealed with shellac. If you are just beginning in silkscreening, a screen that measures 12″ square will be very easy to handle. Starting out with a big screen can be overwhelming, and you would find yourself spending a lot of time cleaning up and using large quantities of ink. In any case, smaller screens are good to practice with.

It takes a lot of organized strength to push a big squeegee properly. Practicing with a smaller squeegee approximately $11\frac{1}{2}″$ will help you get the feel of things. You should also be aware that you need not use the whole area of the screen. Pieces of tracing paper can be used to block out the rest of the screen if you are printing something small, like greeting cards.

If you want to construct your own printing frame, it should be made securely so that it will lie flat on the baseboard and be able to take a lot of lifting up and down as you print. Use wood that is dry and straight. Construct the corners securely, which means that the parts that are to join must be cut accurately. If the corners are sloppy, the screen will not be sturdy.

There are different ways to join the wood. You can cut it at a 45° angle and join the pieces together with 2″ nails. Or, you can use what is known as **bannister stock**—lengths of wood approximately $1\frac{1}{2}″$ on each side—cutting the wood straight across and joining it at right angles with very long nails. You can cut a mortise and tenon joint with a coping saw or a jigsaw and then nail or screw the pieces together. Screws are thought to be more secure than nails, but if the pieces of wood have been cut accurately, nails will suffice. If the screen does wobble after it has been assembled, the best thing would be to take it apart and make sure that the corners have been cut precisely. Metal corner braces can also be used to strengthen the corners after the frame is assembled.

Figure 5.2 Three simple ways of making a printing frame. Here we see (left to right) a butt joint, miter joint, and lap joint. Be sure to cut the wood pieces accurately and join them with long nails.

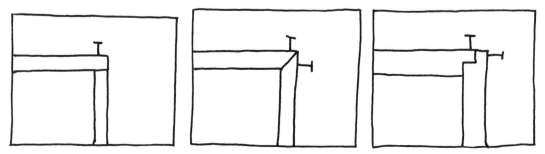

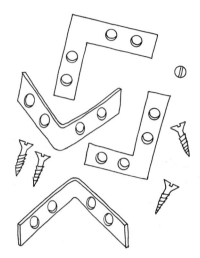

Figure 5.3 Metal corner braces can be used to strengthen weak corners.

A simpler way to make a small frame is to cut a rectangular opening in a piece of $\frac{1}{2}''$ plywood. This way the frame is all in one piece. This is a quick way to make screens that are just the right size for small projects like greeting cards or for use by children. Large scraps of plywood can often be found in the trash, saving you both the time and expense of going to a lumberyard.

Figure 5.4 A group of simple one-piece plywood screen frames.

Once the frame has been assembled, it is stretched very tightly with a piece of SILK, a fabric made especially for silkscreening. Do not confuse this with the silk used for clothing, which is too weak for silkscreening. Silkscreening fabric is extremely strong and can be purchased in an art-supply store that sells materials specifically for silkscreening.

You can also use synthetic silk made from nylon, such as SERACRON. It is slightly less expensive than natural silk, but natural silk is preferable if you want a screen fabric that will readily accept all kinds of film stencils. Photo-film stencils do not adhere well to nylon screens unless the nylon is first treated with a substance such as Ajax cleanser to rough it up a bit.

The silk is woven in different MESHES, ranging in size from 6 to 25. The low numbers indicate a wider, more open weave and the higher numbers, a very close weave. A size 12 is a good all-purpose mesh for most kinds of designs and for printing on most types of paper. The other meshes are useful for more specialized types of printing. Fabric printing, for example, is much easier to do with a screen that has a wider mesh, perhaps a size 8, because the surface of most fabrics is much more absorbent than paper and requires more ink in order to print the stencil clearly.

On the other hand, if a particular design had a lot of HALFTONE dots or very thin lines, then a finer mesh such as size 18 would give the image greater clarity and make it easier to print.

The silk, natural or synthetic, is attached to the frame by using a heavy-duty stapler or a hammer and flat-headed tacks. The silk is stretched bit by bit as you would stretch canvas. Start by tacking the silk to the middle of one side, then tack it to the opposite side. Then do the third and fourth sides. Try to tack all the

Figure 5.5 A hammer and flat-headed tacks or a staple gun can be used to attach the silk securely to the frame.

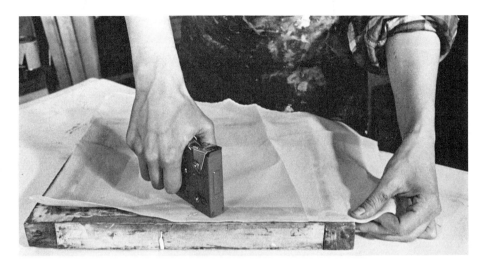

Figure 5.6 The silk is stretched very tightly as it is attached to the frame.

sides gradually, working from the middle out, rather than doing a whole side at one time so that the silk will be stretched evenly. Be sure to pull the silk very tightly as it is being stretched and attached to the screen. There should be no loose, sagging places. Feel the back of the silk with the palm of your hand. It should feel flat. If it feels bumpy, then continue stretching the silk until it does feel smooth. Be sure to allow yourself an ample margin (about 1″ bigger than the outside dimensions of the screen) so that you can get a good grip on the silk as you are stretching it. After the silk has been stretched properly, trim off any excess close to the staples or tacks. Take a hammer and flatten any staples or tacks that are protruding.

Then tape the borders of the frame so that the ink will not leak out in the process of printing. Use the

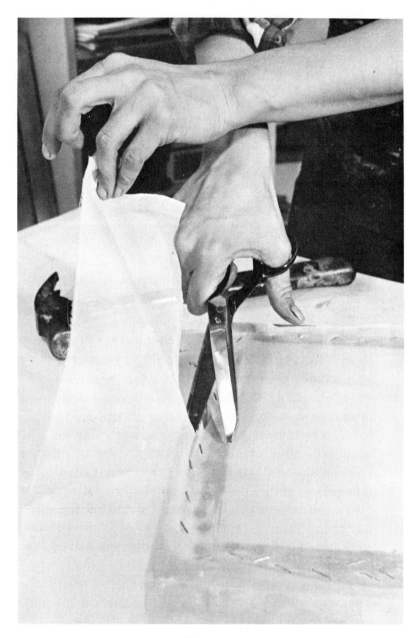

Figure 5.7 The excess silk is trimmed from the frame with scissors.

GUMMED PAPER TAPE moistened with water. Other types of adhesives have an oil base and would dissolve after contact with the ink and paint thinner.

Cut the gummed paper tape into strips according to the outside length and width of the back of the screen and according to the inside dimensions of the screen. The pieces of tape should extend onto the silk about $\frac{1}{2}''$ on the top and sides (where the screen is to be hinged). The bottom of the screen serves as a well for the ink. Here a border of at least $1''$ is necessary so the excess ink won't leak through onto the print. Be sure that the screen is taped on both sides.

The pieces of gummed paper tape should be thoroughly wet and pliable before they are applied to the screen. This can be done by dipping them briefly in a pan of water. After the tape has been secured onto the frame, use a dry rag to mold it to the edges. Be very sure that the strips of tape adhere to both wood and silk.

After the tape has dried, give it two thick coats of SHELLAC. This will make the tape waterproof so that when a film or glue stencil is to be removed with water, the tape will remain undisturbed. Extending the shellac onto the silk by about $\frac{1}{4}''$ will effectively seal the silk to the tape so that no ink, water, or thinner can leak around the edges. Be sure to apply the shellac as thickly as possible for the best protection. If you should spill any shellac on the printing area of the screen, try to wipe it off immediately with some denatured alcohol. Otherwise it will clog the mesh of

Figure 5.8 Use a hammer to make sure that the staples are flat before taping the screen.

Figure 5.9 Cut the strips of gummed paper tape according to the outside and inside dimensions of the frame.

Figure 5.10 The strips of gummed paper tape are dipped into a bowl of water before they are adhered to the frame.

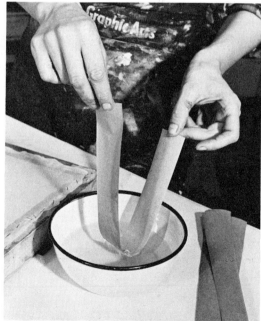

Figure 5.11 The tape strips for the front of the screen are folded as they are molded against the silk and the wood.

Figure 5.12 The gummed paper tape is blotted with a dry rag to make sure it has adhered properly to the frame and lies flat.

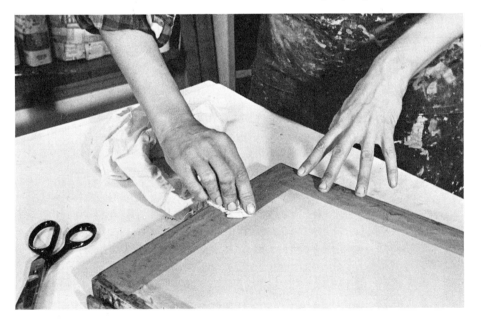

Figure 5.13 The shellac overlaps the tape on both the silk and the wood, providing a secure seal.

the silk and make a spot on whatever you are printing. A good, secure taping will last indefinitely and will save you the trouble of having to retape the screen each time a different color is printed.

The silk itself is very durable if you take good care of it. This means cleaning off the ink as soon as possible—that is, as soon as you have finished printing. You should also be very careful not to let the silk come in contact with any sharp objects which might puncture it. (Watch where you put stencil knives!)

Sometimes after a lot of use, a screen will develop tiny holes. These will probably not affect the quality of the print—especially if they occur in an area that is to be blocked out. If they develop into big holes, then it is time to peel off the tape and replace the old piece of silk.

A baseboard is a flat, smooth piece of wood, such as plywood or masonite, that provides a good surface on which to print. The screen is securely attached to the baseboard with hinges that hold it in the same position

Figure 5.14 This screen is attached to the baseboard with removable pin hinges. A hinge bar is used because the baseboard itself is too thin to take the screws.

throughout the printing. The baseboard should be slightly larger than the size of the screen. You can use the same baseboard for many screens by attaching the screens with removable pin hinges that come apart when the pin is removed. These make it easier to remove glue and film stencils by allowing you to take the screen without the baseboard over to a sink. You can economize on hinges by using one pair on the baseboard and another pair of the same size on the screens. By doing this, two screens can be attached with three hinges.

Attach the screen to the baseboard at the width of the screen. In that way, you can use a shorter squeegee. Be certain that the hinges are screwed in securely so that

Figure 5.15 A screen support loosely attached to the side of the screen holds the screen up while paper is being fed into and removed from the baseboard.

the screen does not wobble or you will have problems in registering or aligning prints. If thin wood or masonite is being used as a baseboard, it will be necessary to use a HINGE BAR—a piece of wood as thick as the screen frame—to have something thick enough to sink the screws into. The hinge bar is nailed to the baseboard at the width, and then the actual hinge is attached.

The screen and baseboard are ready for action when a SCREEN SUPPORT is attached to the side of the screen. This is a strip of wood, approximately 5″ long, that is loosely attached to the left-hand side of the screen. It swings down automatically when the screen is lifted and supports the screen when you take it off the baseboard while hanging up your prints and feeding new sheets of paper on the baseboard. If the screen is not supported, the ink might leak down to the baseboard and ruin the print.

The SQUEEGEE is the last piece of equipment you will need (see Figure 5.1). This is the tool that squeezes the ink evenly through the mesh of the silk onto the paper or fabric underneath. You should buy a squeegee with a rubber blade about $\frac{5}{8}$″ thick. Thinner blades do not provide good pressure or an even distribution of ink. They also tend to wiggle and produce blurry prints.

A squeegee works best if the blade is kept sharp, that is, if the two edges of the blade remain squared. After a lot of use, these edges will tend to become rounded. They can be resquared by rubbing the squeegee back and forth on a piece of very fine sandpaper, being sure to keep the squeegee in an upright, perpendicular position.

A good-quality squeegee is quite durable. The blade is made of special-grade rubber that is not affected by the ink or by the cleaning solvents. Be careful that the blade does not get nicked or accumulate dried ink. Clean the squeegee when you clean the screen—as soon as you are finished printing. Wipe off the ink with a cardboard square, a rag, and paint thinner.

A squeegee should be $\frac{1}{2}''$ smaller than the inside width of the screen. This allows you to print the entire area of the screen without having to overlap strokes, which would leave a streak of heavy ink on the surface of the print.

However, if you are only going to print with a small area of your screen, it will be much more convenient to use a smaller squeegee. If you do not have one, a piece of rigid cardboard will do for a very small design. It will be less tiring for you than pulling a big squeegee, **and** it is disposable.

Squeegees should be stored carefully in a place where the blade won't get bumped. Metal cup hooks screwed into the ends of the handle are handy for hanging them up so they will be out of the way.

INK, COLORS, MIXING, AND CLEANING

Silkscreening uses the brightest and most beautiful colors. It is impossible to be unenthusiastic about them. The specially developed inks used in silkscreening are, for the most part, oil base and are known as **poster inks.** Colors dry in about 15 minutes, which allows for quick overprinting. Poster inks work well on paper and cardboard, drying with a flat matte finish.

Because these inks are oil base, they require careful handling. Cleaning up is done with a solvent (SCREEN WASH)—PAINT THINNER, MINERAL SPIRITS, or TURPENTINE. (Paint thinner is the cheapest.) Soap and water do **not** help in cleaning off oil-base inks; in fact they only make things messier. To see exactly what dissolves what, refer to Appendix C.

Working with ink can be either a joyous experience, as you mix delicious colors and discover new ones, or it can be extremely frustrating. How you react depends on how organized you are about it. I happen to love mixing ink and the way it smells and feels, but I realize that not everyone will be as enthusiastic about this as I am.

Whenever you are planning to mix some ink, make sure that you have some empty jars, rags, spoons,

Figure 6.1 Cans and jars of ink are kept handy and accessible on open shelves.

paint thinner, and newspaper handy. It is sometimes helpful to take the phone off the hook to eliminate interruptions. Never mix ink in a hurry. Take your time. Experiment until you find the color you want. The range is limitless. Relax and enjoy working with the ink—you can always clean your hands afterwards.

As you will see from looking at the color plates in this book, ink can have many characteristics: it can be opaque (thick) or transparent (thin), or anything in between. It can be glossy or dull. Ink of different qualities can also be combined in a single print. It is possible to print a thick ink on top of other colors and completely cover these colors. Or to overprint transparent colors so as to pick up the colors beneath them and create new colors. A thick white can be printed on black stock, and it will remain white. A transparent white on black stock will become light gray. Transparent colors can be used like thin watercolor washes, where each additional color that is printed produces a new shade in the overlapping areas—with no extra stencil. For example, a transparent magenta shape overlapped on a transparent blue shape will create the sensation of purple. This can be compared with overlapping pieces of transparent plastic.

Silkscreen colors come in individual cans. All the colors are intermixable, and the cans can be bought in different sizes. A basic assortment would be composed of the most brilliant colors on the color chart—such as fire red, magenta, cadmium yellow, emerald green, peacock blue, and cerise—plus black and white. Although the exact names of these colors may vary, remember to get the most brilliant colors to allow for the greatest flexibility in mixing to produce all the other shades.

A brilliant color can always be made duller if you wish. This is usually done by adding a small amount of its opposite color (explained later in this chapter). However, a bright color can never be produced by mixing—you have to start out with the bright color.

For example, if you take yellow and blue and try to mix them together to produce a vivid emerald green, you will always wind up with a dull, calm green no matter what proportions of color you use.

I t will be helpful to explain briefly how colors are organized and their relationship to each other. Traditionally, colors have been divided into the **primary colors** of red, blue, and yellow and the **secondary colors** of green, purple, and orange. The primary colors supposedly mix among themselves to produce the secondary colors. These six colors are usually arranged in a circle known as a **color wheel,** a diagram much like a pie with six slices (see Figure 6.2). If the colors were laid out in a straight line you would have a color spectrum or rainbow.

Silkscreen colors conform roughly to this color wheel. Red and yellow will produce an orange when mixed,

Figure 6.2 Color wheel. The primary colors of yellow, red, and blue mix to form the secondary colors of orange, green, and purple.

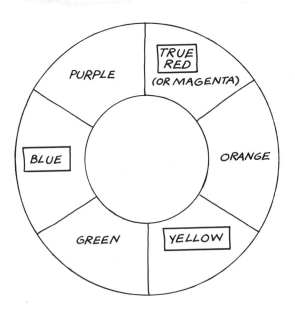

but not like the bright, intense orange sold in the can. Another difference is that silkscreen red cannot be mixed with blue to form a satisfactory purple. Since it is not a pure red, but has an admixture of orange, mixing it with blue produces a muddy brown color. If you want to get purple or lavender shades, the proper color to mix with blue is magenta, a **true** red with no orange. This is really a basic color, used a great deal for silkscreening.

If you want to make a color duller, that is, less intense, you can add a little bit of the color opposite it on the color wheel. If you want an orange that is not so bright, add a little blue to it. Adding a little bit of black to a color will also dull it. Adding white to a color will tint it or make it lighter. White added to purple will produce a lavender color.

It is impossible to describe exactly what proportions of various colors to use or to give precise formulas for specific results. Color is a very personal thing. The only way you will find the colors you really want is to experiment. Try mixing samples of color on a palette. Experiment with a number of color combinations until you find those you like and consider well suited to the particular design you are planning to print.

The colors in the cans are highly concentrated, that is, they are thick and opaque. They should always be mixed with some TRANSPARENT BASE in order to achieve the right consistency for silkscreening. Transparent base is a colorless gel that looks a lot like Vaseline. Always be sure you have a sufficient amount of transparent base on hand when mixing ink; if you use the colors right out of the can, you will find it hard to work the squeegee, and the ink will tend to clog the open areas of the screen. In addition, unthinned ink will dry too fast on the screen and be very difficult to clean. Paint thinner, despite its name, will not thin the ink satisfactorily because it is a liquid. It will merely make the ink too drippy.

The ink should be thoroughly mixed with transparent base **before** it is poured on the screen; otherwise the color will be streaky. Use a ceramic bowl or a palette and a palette knife to mix the ink.

If you add about 20 percent base to a color, it will still remain opaque. If you want a more transparent color, the proportion of base to color should be increased. The more base you use, the more transparent the color will be.

Transparent colors can also be mixed from artists' oil colors, such as Grumbacher or Windsor Newton. The oil colors are mixed directly from the tube with transparent base. It is best to use a flat surface such as a palette, a piece of glass, or a formica counter area. The colors in the tubes, like those in cans, are very concentrated and if they are not well mixed with the

Above: *Go Slo,* Corita Kent, 1963. Four cut tracing-paper stencils were used.

Right: *Valentine 10,* Maria Termini, 1970. Cut paper stencils.

Below: *Night Song,* Maria Termini, 1976. Two torn paper stencils were printed on green charcoal paper with overlapping transparent colors.

Rainbowtree, Maria Termini, 1974. Cut paper stencils.

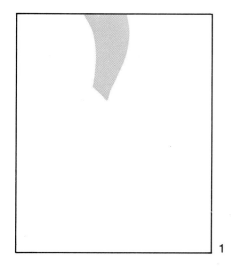

1

2

3

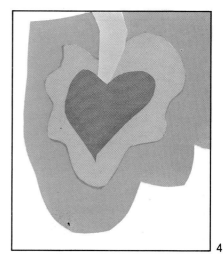

4

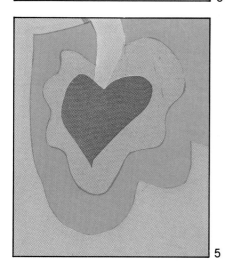

5

Color proofs of *Valentine 10,* Maria Termini, 1970.

1 The first color, gold, is printed. Its shape is cut a bit bigger than it actually will be because the other colors overlap. These undercuts, or traps, are very important if all the colors are to lock together properly.
2 The second color, green, is printed. Notice how it overlaps the gold.
3 The third color, pink, is printed, overlapping the gold and green.
4 The fourth color, blue, is printed, slightly overlapping the other colors.
5 The fifth color, purple, is printed, overlapping the blue and gold.
The overlaps are almost invisible when opaque inks are used.

Above: *OK,* Maria Termini, 1975.
Torn and cut paper stencils.

Left: *Eclipse 8,* Maria Termini, 1970.
Cut paper stencils.

Opposite: *Collage 10,* Maria Termini,
1970. Torn paper stencils with
overlapping transparent colors.

Left: *Moonplant No. 4.,* Maria Termini. Cut paper stencils.

Below: *Hot Guitar,* Maria Termini, 1974. Cut paper stencils.

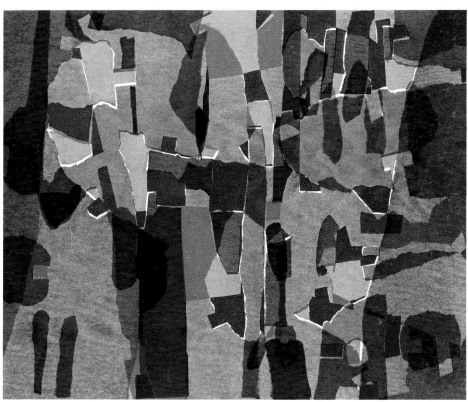

Left: *Passion Flower No. 1,* Maria Termini, 1975. Cut paper stencils.

Below: *Skywriting,* Maria Termini, 1975. Progressive glue stencil.

Opposite: *Parakeet Rhapsody, No. 1,* Marja Lianko-Roberts, 1976. Glue stencil via resists. Lithographic crayon (stick tusche) was used to produce the surface texture by rubbing corrugated cardboard and masonite through the screen. Liquid tusche produced the brush strokes. The stencils were printed with blended colors to produce a floating image.

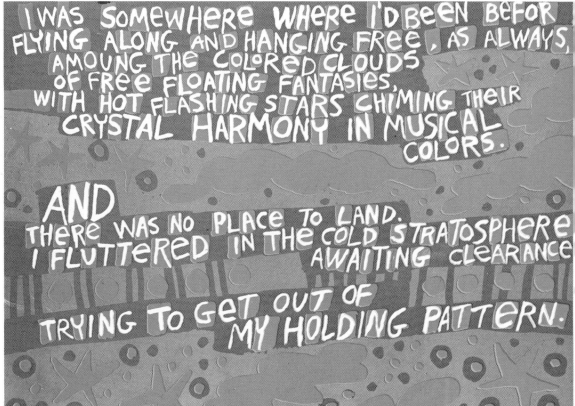

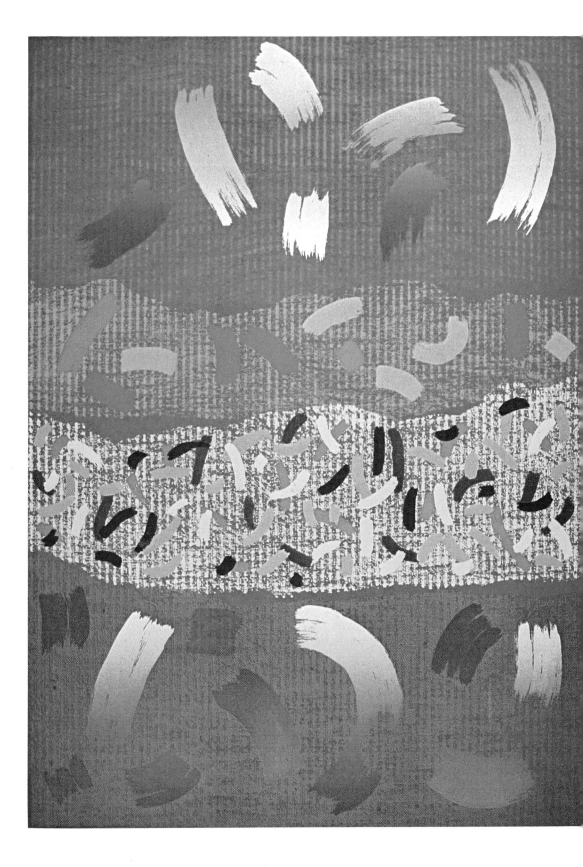

1

Progressive color proofs of *Striped Heart*, Maria Termini, 1976.

2

3

4

1 A medium-pink background color is printed first. The overall shape with rounded corners is masked on the screen with glue.

2 A green heart is printed on top of the pink, using a cut paper stencil. The glue mask from the previous color remains on the screen. (The paper stencil will be used again for the last step.)

3 Stripes of glue are painted over the glue window on the screen. Orange stripes are overprinted on the whole area of the print.

4 The glue stripes remain on the screen, and the paper stencil is used to mask out everything except the heart, which is overprinted with purple stripes to cover the orange stripes.

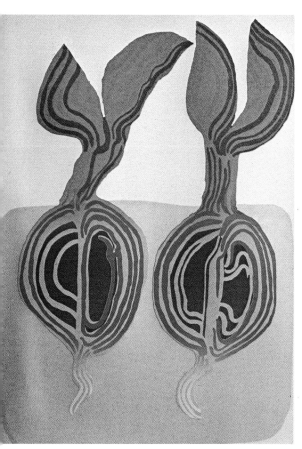

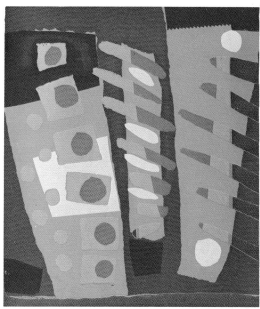

Below: *Magic Peas,* Maria Termini, 1975. Paper and glue stencils.

Above: *Birth,* Bonita Barlow, 1975. Progressive glue method. The large seed shapes were progressively blocked out and overprinted in the various colors, sometimes squeegeed with more than one color on the screen to produce the shading within the shapes. A final printing of a very lightly tinted overprint varnish provided background. The print became glossy where the varnish went over the inked areas and remained matte in the other areas.

Right: *The Path in the Rain,* Maria Termini, 1976. Paper and glue stencils.

1

Progressive proofs of *No Smoking,*
Maria Termini, 1975.

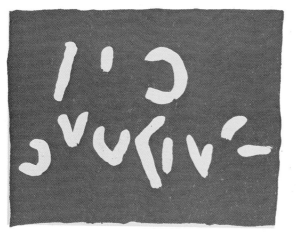

2

3

1 A yellow rectangle is printed first as a
background.
2 Part of the letters are painted on the screen
with glue. Then this stencil is overprinted on the
yellow rectangle with pink.
3 More glue is added to the same screen to
complete the letters. This new stencil is printed
over the pink in purple. Where the glue had been
added, the print remains pink.
4 More glue is added around the edges of the
letters and in the middle of each "O" where
green is overprinted.

4

Left: *Bel Paese, No. 5,* Maria Termini, 1976. Progressive glue stencil. The first color was a solid-yellow rectangle.

Below: *Scherzo,* Maria Termini, 1976. Progressive glue stencil. First a solid-red rectangle was printed. Then some glue dots were painted on the screen and the stencil was overprinted with a medium pink onto the red. Then more glue dots were added and the stencil was printed in a medium blue over the medium pink.

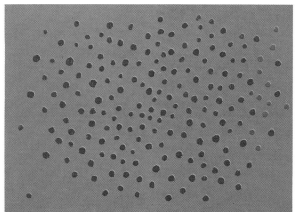

Garden in the Sky, Maria Termini, 1976. Progressive glue stencil.

Below: *A Little Dab'll Do Ya,* Paula Latos-Valier, 1973. Paper and hand-cut film stencils.

Right: *Call Me Up When You're Down,* Maria Termini, 1975. Progressive glue stencil.

Bottom: *Silver Top Diner,* Biron Valier, 1973. A combination of paper stencils for the larger areas and hand-cut film stencils for the smaller areas.

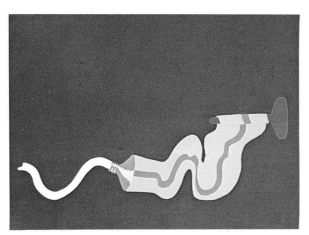

The Wandering Eye, Micaela Myers, 1973. Cut tracing-paper stencils and photo stencils.

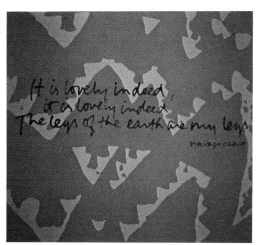

Above: *The Legs of the Earth Are My Legs,* Corita Kent, 1976. Two photo stencils, one from a greatly enlarged section of a shell and the other from the enlarged handwriting of the artist, were printed over a colored background.

Right: *Wendy's Garden,* Micaela Myers and Wendy King (age 9), 1973. A combination of a photo stencil produced from the original drawing by Wendy and hand-cut tracing-paper stencils for the individual colors.

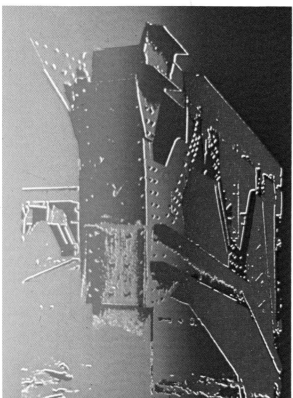

Above: *Negative Foliage,* Tim Hamill, 1971. Printed from four tone separations (high-contrast positives of different exposure times) made from the same black–and–white negative.

Left: *Structure No. 4,* Victoria Porras. Two photo stencils, one from a high-contrast positive and the other from a high-contrast negative of the same image, were printed slightly off register to produce the white outline around most of the image. The shaded color was produced by printing each stencil with several colors at the same time.

Opposite: *Paleontologist's Dream,* Tim Hamill, 1971. A combination of photo, glue, and hand-cut film stencils.

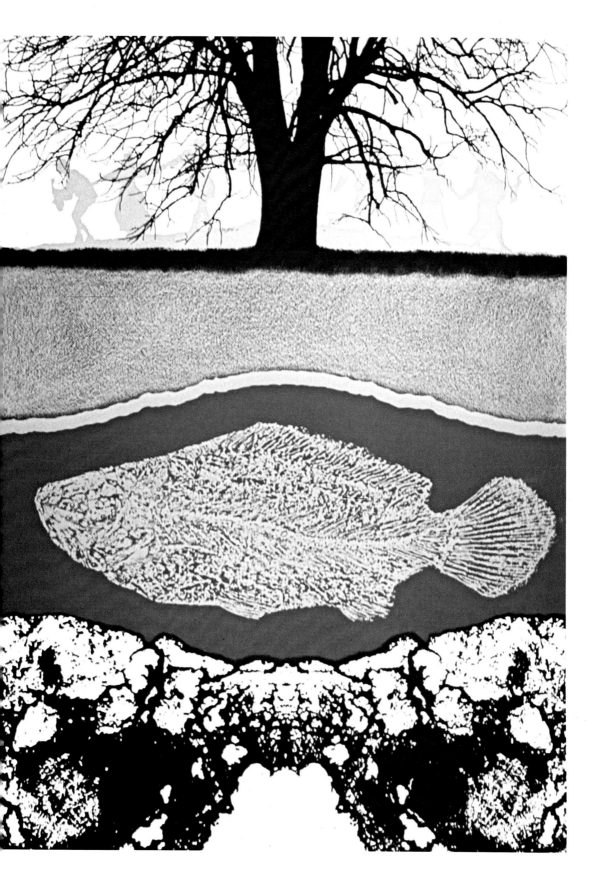

Left: *Modular Pholage,* Tim Hamill, 1969. A section of a mural in a Boston restaurant. Small squares of painted plywood were screened with stencils produced from high-contrast and line images from architecture and art sources.

Below: *Safed,* Maria Termini, 1976. Two high-contrast positives of different exposure times produced two different stencils, each of which was printed over the background color.

Figure 6.3 Mixing ink and transparent base in a round-bottomed bowl.

Figure 6.4 Tube oil colors and base can be mixed to form transparent colors using a palette and a knife with a flexible blade.

base, you will get streaks on the print. It is hard to judge exactly how transparent a color is, but you can get a good approximation by smudging a bit of the color on a piece of the printing paper.

The ink—both that in the cans and that which you mix yourself and put in jars—can be stored indefinitely, providing it is in a well-sealed container. Be sure that the rims of the cans are clean of ink before they are resealed. If you keep ink in glass jars be sure that the lids screw on tightly. A strip of masking tape around the lid will make a better seal if you plan to store the ink for a long time. Avoid storing it in plastic containers, since ink often dissolves plastic.

Poster inks are recommended for all kinds of paper and cardboard. They are also available in a glossy finish and in metallic and fluorescent colors. There are

Figure 6.5 Jars of ink with screw-top lids. Sealing the lids with masking tape will make them more secure.

many specialized types of ink for such surfaces as glass, plastic, and metal, which are specially formulated to adhere well to these types of surfaces. Fabric ink, in particular, must have a much finer formulation than poster ink if it is to penetrate the fibers of the fabric.

You can get more detailed information about other inks from your silkscreen supplier. This information is very important because some inks require special solvents and can only be used with certain types of stencils.

Silkscreen inks that are water-soluble are also available for printing on paper. The advantage of such inks is that they eliminate the time-consuming cleanup with paint thinner. However, these inks must be washed out very quickly or they will dry in the screen, and they also have an increased tendency to clog the stencil. Obviously, they are not the answer to all cleaning problems. If you are not working near a sink, washing away water-base inks can be a problem.

There are other limitations with water-base inks; for example, you can only use certain kinds of stencils. Glue stencils and the easy-to-use film stencils are water-soluble and would be dissolved by these water-base inks. Another disadvantage is that they tend to wrinkle the paper, making close REGISTRATION very difficult. As mentioned, oil-base inks can be removed

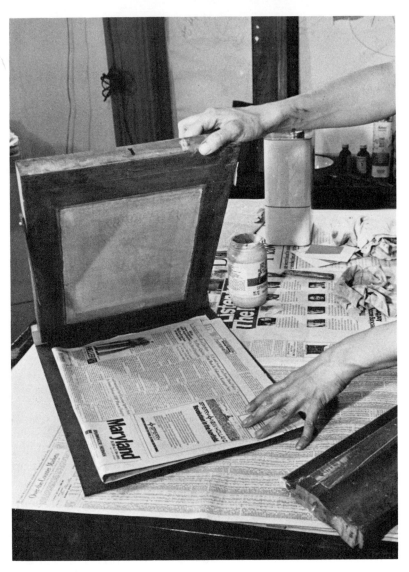

Figure 6.6 Sheets of newspaper are placed under the screen.

from the screen with a number of solvents, such as paint thinner, kerosene, mineral spirits, or turpentine. In addition to being the least expensive, paint thinner is readily available in any hardware store. As soon as you are finished printing, the screen should be cleaned. Waiting will only give the ink a chance to dry up.

Be organized about cleaning. This means that before you start printing you should have assembled within reach everything you need to clean up efficiently: lots of rags cut up in small, easy-to-handle pieces, paint thinner, cardboard squares, newspaper, and a trash can.

Begin by putting a piece of newspaper under the screen. The screen can remain attached to the baseboard. Paper stencils should be peeled off when the screen is being cleaned; other kinds of stencils can be left on the screen throughout the cleaning. Any ink left on the screen should be scraped off with a cardboard square and put back into the jar or can. It can be used again, as long as it is not lumpy from having partially dried out.

After you have scraped off all the ink you can, pour some paint thinner on the screen and swish it around with a rag to dissolve the ink. You can let the screen soak for a minute or so while you clean off the squeegee.

After the solvent has had time to work, lift the screen, take dry rags, and wipe it. If all the ink has not been removed, use more newspaper and repeat the application of paint thinner until the screen can be wiped clean. After the screen has been wiped clean of the thinner, you should be able to look through the mesh and see if there are any particles of dried ink still clogging the mesh. The mesh must be clear to produce good-quality prints.

Figure 6.7 The leftover ink can be salvaged from the screen by scraping it up with a small cardboard square.

Figure 6.8 Paint thinner is poured onto the screen, and a rag is used to rub the thinner into the mesh of the silk to dissolve the remaining ink.

Figure 6.9 The screen is wiped dry with a clean rag to find out whether or not the mesh of the screen is clear.

Figure 6.10 A cardboard square easily scrapes the ink left on the squeegee right back into the jar or can.

If further applications of paint thinner do not remove these clogged spots, a stronger solvent such as a nondetergent type BRUSH CLEANER should be used. Try not to get the brush cleaner near the shellacked border or it will eat away at the shellac. Pour the brush cleaner sparingly on a rag and apply it to the trouble spots.

Brush cleaner or lacquer thinner can also be very handy if you are using a new screen that is not yet broken in. If you want to print a light color such as yellow right after having printed a very dark color, you can finish cleaning the screen by wiping the silk with some brush cleaner or lacquer thinner. This effectively removes all traces of the previous color so that is won't bleed through onto the next color. Bleeding occurs only with new screens; as a screen gets a lot of use you can print from light to dark with no problems.

The trick to cleaning up fast is to have a large supply of rags handy. Ask your friends to save them for you. If you live in an apartment building, you might put up a sign near the mailboxes asking people to call you if they have old clothes, sheets, or towels that they are planning to get rid of. You can use paper towels if you have no rags, but they are not nearly as absorbent.

Rags soaked with paint and thinner should be discarded or stored in a place where they will not be prone to spontaneous combustion. They are **extremely flammable,** as are the inks, so keep them in a cool, well-ventilated place far away from sparks and cigarette ashes. And, please don't smoke where silkscreening is being done.

As for cleaning yourself up, Goop or other waterless hand cleaner will do a good job of getting the ink off your hands without drying your skin. This type of cleaner uses the heat of your hands to dissolve the ink.

Figure 6.11 A waterless hand cleaner, such as Goop, will remove ink from your hands without drying them.

SETTING UP A WORK SPACE

Silkscreening can be done almost anywhere. There is no need for a lot of bulky equipment. However, there are a few things to consider about the space you will work in.

The room should have some kind of ventilation—a window that can be easily opened or a fan to draw the air out. Sometimes the fumes from the ink and thinner can be quite strong.

It would be nice to have a separate room especially for silkscreening, but in reality most people don't and can't. Although it's great to be able to leave everything set up where other family members or roommates cannot disturb things, you may have to be content with silkscreening in an area where a lot of other activities take place—in the kitchen, a corner of the dining room, and so on. There's nothing impossible about this arrangement. Basements can also be nice to work in, usually peaceful and not in a high-traffic area.

A large, sturdy table is an absolute necessity. It should be of a height that will be comfortable for you while working standing up. It should be strong and not prone to wobbling. Card tables should be used only if they are the last tables left on earth. Two saw horses and a sheet of thick plywood will make a cheap, sturdy table.

Good lighting is also essential in the area where you will be working on stencils and printing. Try to

Figure 7.1 A large, sturdy table used for printing.

Figure 7.2 A pegboard holds squeegees, rolls of tape, and small tools.

arrange adequate shelf space for storing ink and other supplies: old kitchen cabinets or planks and cinderblocks work fine. Try to hang up your squeegees, both to prevent damage to them and to have them immediately at hand. A piece of pegboard is handy for small tools and rolls of tape. You can use some wide shelves as a flat storage area for paper, screens, and finished prints. Heavy cardboard portfolios, which can be bought or made in any size, are also ideal for storage purposes. Extra screens should be covered with cardboard when you store them so that there will be less chance of something puncturing the silk.

When you begin running off a large number of prints, it will be important to have some kind of system for hanging wet prints. You can make a simple, efficient drying line by drilling holes in the flat ends of

Figure 7.3 Clothespins strung on a line can each hold two wet prints back to back.

wooden clothespins and stringing them on a length of strong line. Then attach the line to opposite walls at a convenient height. The line can be removed when it's not in use so people won't bump into it, and it's an economical way to hang many prints in a small space. With the clothespins strung this way, two wet prints can be hung in one pin. In fact, fifty prints can be hung on 25 pins on about a yard of clothesline. Install the line as close to your printing table as possible so as to eliminate your having to walk back and forth. Clothespins can also be nailed to long strips of wood, and these strips can be hinged to the wall in such a way that you can lift them up and out of the way when not in use. Commercial printing plants often use big drying racks of wood or metal. These, however, are expensive and take up a lot of floor space.

Access to running water is necessary to remove glue and film stencils. If you can, work near the kitchen or bathroom. A stereo or radio can be a good companion and provide a more enjoyable working atmosphere.

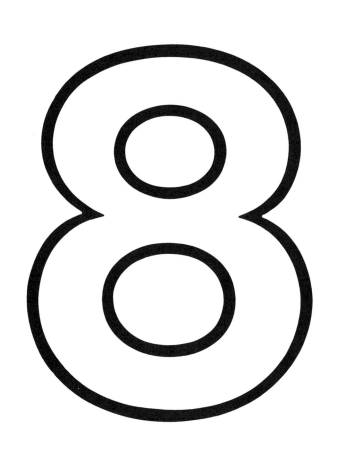

LAYOUTS AND REGISTRATION

Silkscreening is easier if you are able to plan ahead and organize. Never underestimate the power of thinking ahead, especially in the areas of **layout** and **registration.**

A LAYOUT is an actual-size sketch of what you plan to print. REGISTRATION is the process of aligning the different colors in a single print.

Most often a layout is simply a pencil-outline drawing of the shapes that you are going to print, although it can be more precise. It should indicate what colors are to go where, with the names of the

Figure 8.1 A layout for a five-color print with butt registration. The color areas are indicated by a line drawing, with each color name labelled. The margin is also indicated. Because the colors touch each other, they are printed in sequence from light to dark—gold, light olive, pink, light blue, and medium purple.

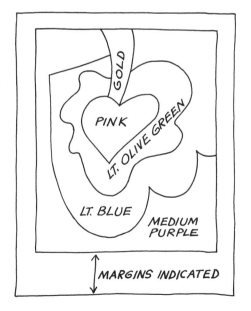

colors penciled directly on the shapes. It is not necessary to color in all the areas of the design or to make separate drawings for each color. This would make the registration confusing. In silkscreening, the alignment of colors is simplified by cutting stencils as they are printed. Print the first color right on the layout; then, using that as an accurate guide, cut the stencil for the next color.

Use the layout as a running guide for making the stencils by placing tracing paper and hand-cut stencils over the layout and using an X-acto knife to trace and remove the shapes that are to be printed. If you are using a glue stencil, the silk is usually sufficiently transparent that the layout can be seen when placed underneath on the baseboard. In the photo-stencil method, layouts are made from HIGH-CONTRAST POSITIVES and black ink on ACETATE. These are then used, much like a negative, to photographically produce an image on the photo-stencil film.

To avoid confusion, work up your layout on a piece of paper the same size you are planning to use for your prints. This will show you the precise relationships among the various colors and shapes, lines and letters. You should be able to determine how many stencils you will need. Usually each color requires a separate stencil, especially if the colors touch one another. However, there are two exceptions to this.

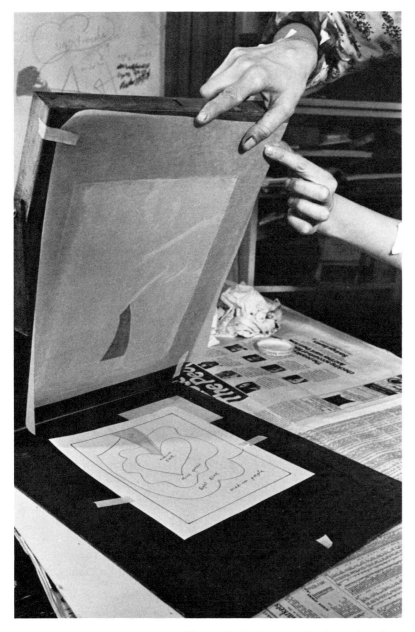

Figure 8.2 Always print the colors first on the layout, which can then be used as a very accurate guide when forming stencils for the other colors.

If transparent overlapping colors are used, a new color can be created where the shapes meet. This is considered a **free color**—that is, it is not printed by itself.

If you are using a glue or film stencil and you have different colored lines and shapes that are separated by a lot of unprinted space, then it is possible to put more than one color on the same stencil. Simply block out one color with tracing paper while you are printing the other.

Some layouts are easier to do than others. Overlapping transparent shapes and shapes that are fairly distant from each other are not complicated to print. The registration is accomplished by feeding the paper into the same position on the baseboard, and the shapes can be cut exactly as they are to appear.

The most-difficult kind of layout is one in which the shapes touch each other. This is known as BUTT REGISTRATION (see Figure 8.1). In this type of layout, the colors should be printed from light to dark. The shapes are slightly overlapped on each other with no noticeable effect, since the darker colors cover the lighter ones. With butt registration, it is very important to allow for TRAPS—that is, for undercuts and overcuts. The shapes of the lighter colors have to be cut and printed a little bit bigger than they will actually appear (UNDERLAPS). The subsequently

Figure 8.3 In this print—*Buon Natale,* by the author—none of the colors touch. Hence, they could be printed in any sequence.

printed, darker colors are also cut to overlap the lighter colors. In this way the shapes will lock together perfectly with no intervening white spaces between them. This type of registration is **extremely** dependent on the constant correct positioning of the paper in the **register corner** on the baseboard every time a color is printed.

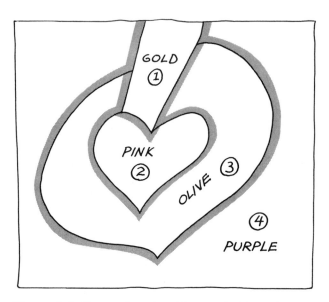

Figure 8.4 Butt registration. Here, as in Figure 8.1, the colors slightly overlap each other in the shaded areas to ensure a perfect fit. Since the color sequence is from light to dark, this overlap is not visible.

The REGISTER CORNER is a corner formed at a precise right angle on the baseboard with three or four thicknesses of masking tape. Its position is determined by the size of the paper being used. The register corner ensures that the printing paper will be fed into the same position each time a color is being printed, and thus enables you to add other colors to the print in correct alignment.

Another type of layout involves large background shapes on which smaller shapes or lines are superimposed. Here you should print the larger shapes

Figure 8.5 A corner of masking tape indicates the precise spot on the baseboard into which the paper is fed. This register corner is necessary for aligning multiple-color prints.

first and then overprint the smaller elements. The single, most important thing in the entire procedure is to be accurate about feeding the paper into the register corner. It takes some practice to be consistent—do not get discouraged. Remember that if the position of the printing paper has shifted, the color printed will not be in the same position on every print and the other colors also will be slightly off.

Use both hands to position the paper into the corner. If you use your left elbow to keep the screen in a raised position, both hands will be free to feed the paper into the corner. Also be sure that the screen is securely attached to the baseboard so that the hinges are not loose. Otherwise, the screen itself will move and your color areas will vary in position from print to print.

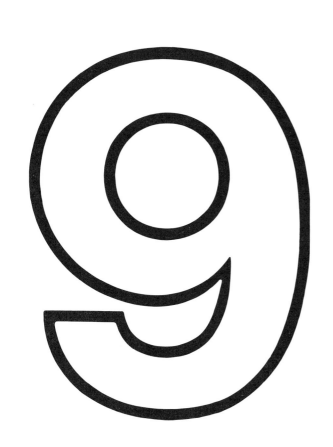

If you are beginning to silkscreen, you will surely find paper stencils the easiest to work with. They are quick, simple, economical, and durable. Paper stencils have been greatly underrated. They are actually amazingly strong: you can print as many copies as you want, even up to 300. Of course, the entire quantity must be completed in one printing, because the paper stencil has to be removed for cleaning the ink from the screen. You will see the wide variety of prints that can be made from paper stencils in the color section of this book.

A paper stencil is made from any kind of thin paper. TRACING PAPER works well because it is transparent and can easily be cut with a knife. Attached under the silk, the paper prevents the ink from going through the mesh. The natural tackiness of the ink is sufficient to adhere the paper stencil to the silk. The paper is cut with an X-acto knife according to the layout. Torn paper shapes can also be used as stencils to produce a rough-edged effect. Shapes can be arranged on a sheet of printing paper under the screen in position on the baseboard. They will stick to the screen after the first print has been squeegeed.

Paper stencils are well suited for designs that involve fairly large-size shapes, that is, shapes that can be easily cut or torn.

The best place to cut paper stencils is right on the baseboard of your screen. Raise the screen out of the way on its hinges while you are working on the stencil.

Begin by positioning the layout on the baseboard where it should fit comfortably. Check to be sure that your design will fit within the area of the screen. If you measure this area before you start drawing the layout, you won't wind up designing something that is too big for your screen. Do the layout on a piece of printing paper and be sure to indicate where the margins are to be.

Tape the layout lightly to the baseboard with two small pieces of tape so that it will remain stationary. Then establish and tape down the register corner with

Figure 9.1 A layout held in position on the baseboard by two small pieces of tape.

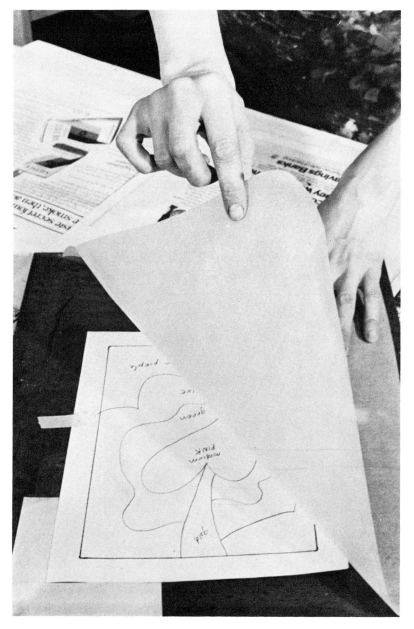

Figure 9.2 The layout has been covered with tracing paper, which is also secured to the baseboard with tape.

masking tape. This should be done at an exact right angle conforming to the upper-right-hand corner of the printing paper. This same corner can be used over and over again with different paper stencils if you are printing on the same-size paper.

Next take a piece of tracing paper big enough to cover the screen completely, and tape it over the layout. Then, cut out and remove the tracing paper in those areas that are to be printed. Be sure your knife has a sharp blade so you'll get clean edges. Don't worry about loose floating parts. Just let them remain in position on the layout. The ink will pick them up and hold them to the screen with the main part of the stencil.

Figure 9.3 The tracing paper is being cut with an X-acto knife. The parts that are to be printed are removed.

If you are using <u>butt registration</u>, be sure to plan ahead: cut the shapes for the lighter colors slightly larger than their actual size. The other colors will then overlap the lighter ones by a slight margin, but the printing sequence from light to dark will make this overlap invisible. If you have a layout in which none of the colors touch, the sequence is optional.

When you are ready to print, remove the pieces of tape that are holding the stencil to the baseboard. Be very careful not to disturb the position of the stencil once it is correctly lined up with the master sketch. If you have any loose floating parts, let them remain in position in the layout. Bring the screen down on top of the stencil and the layout, with the layout still on the baseboard. Do your first print on it. Then, use it as an accurate cutting guide for the stencils that are to follow.

Mix up the color you want, being sure to use some transparent base to make it a good screening consistency. Pour a thick ribbon of ink about 1″ wide at the bottom of the screen on the width closest to you and away from the hinges. If you are printing a lot of prints, you will probably add more ink as it gets used up. Keep in mind that having too much ink on the screen can get sloppy.

Figure 9.4 The pieces of tape that hold the stencil to the baseboard are removed carefully without disturbing the position of the stencil.

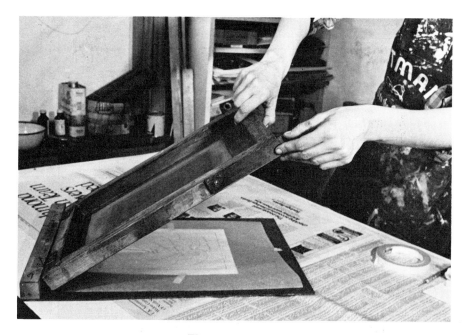

Figure 9.5 The screen is lowered onto the paper stencil and printing can begin. The layout remains on the baseboard, and the first print is done right on it.

Figure 9.6 A line of ink is poured along the bottom of the screen.

Hold the squeegee firmly with both hands. Pick up the ink on the blade that is facing you. Pull the ink all the way from the top to the bottom of the screen with firm, even pressure. The ink will go through the open spaces of the paper stencil and produce a corresponding image on the paper beneath the screen.

After you have pulled the first print, carefully lift the screen up from the baseboard. The paper stencil will be attached to the silk as if it were glued. It will

Figure 9.7 The ink is picked up with the blade of the squeegee facing you. The ink is pulled from the top (the end near the hinges) to the bottom of the screen. Pulling the first print will cause the stencil to adhere to the silk.

Figure 9.8 The screen is carefully lifted up. The tackiness of the ink will cause the stencil to adhere to the silk.

stay this way for as many prints as you wish to print. Tape the corners of the stencil to the frame with masking tape so they won't flap around. Remove the layout from the baseboard and proceed to print. Remember to keep the layout as a guide for cutting the second and all subsequent stencils. The advantage of this system is its accuracy—you know exactly where the previous colors are, since they have already been printed directly on the layout.

As long as the stencil stays flat and wrinkle free, an almost unlimited number of prints can be printed. However, they must be printed at one time and the ink must be kept moving so that it will not begin to dry

Figure 9.9 The corners of the stencil are taped to the frame after the stencil is adhered.

and clog the screen. As we have already noted, <u>if there is some clogging, a rag with a little bit of paint thinner applied to the open areas of the stencil will help clear the mesh of ink.</u>

As you print, be very careful to feed the paper precisely into the register corner to ensure good alignment. This is particularly important with butt registration, as mentioned in Chapter 8.

Good squeegee technique involves firm, even pressure. Usually the squeegee forms a 45° angle to the silk. Sometimes two complete pulls of the squeegee are necessary to get a clear print, that is, to ensure penetration of the ink through all the open areas of the stencil. Try to keep the ink moving in one direction only, from top to bottom of the screen. This results in the firmest pressure possible, which produces a sharp print. If you happen to miss part of your design, then simply reposition the print in the register corner and overprint it.

When the application of the ink is complete after squeegeeing, lift the screen up from the baseboard **quickly.** The print will automatically separate from the screen. If the paper does not release as you lift the screen, simply peel it off the screen. Meanwhile the

Figure 9.10 The screen can be supported with the left elbow, leaving both hands free to feed the paper into the register corner accurately.

squeegee can rest comfortably on the silk against the top edge of the screen while you are hanging your print and feeding in paper.

To avoid getting smudges on your prints, be sure that your hands stay clean. The trick here is to keep the squeegee handle free of ink. Keep a good supply of rags handy.

When you have finished printing, scrape off as much ink as possible with a cardboard square. Then lift up the screen, peel off the paper stencil, and proceed to clean the screen with paint thinner.

Paper stencils do not always have to be done exactly as planned from a layout. Torn paper shapes can be arranged on a piece of paper on the baseboard, just as you would arrange a collage. These shapes will stick on the screen when you pull the first print. If your printing paper is smaller than the screen or if you want to have a border around the print, make a mask of tracing paper on the silk.

Working with torn paper shapes is a very free way of working. It is a lot like painting in that colors and shapes are determined by what has already been printed. Torn paper shapes can even be moved around on the screen until you have an arrangement that is satisfying. Remember that where there is paper, no ink will go through.

Figure 9.11 Paper stencils are simply peeled off the screen before cleaning up with paint thinner.

Figure 9.12 Torn paper shapes are arranged on a piece of printing paper. The ink will adhere them to the screen.

As you gain experience, try experimenting with other kinds of paper for stencils: WAX PAPER, computer tape, newspaper, and tissue paper. Using absorbent paper towels as stencils can give the effect of a solid color and a lighter shade of the same color as some of the ink bleeds through the paper towel. Typewritten words can be printed using a mimeograph stencil cut on a typewriter. Attach the mimeograph stencil to the underside of the screen with masking tape and proceed to print.

Printing with paper stencils will help you experience and develop some basic silkscreen skills. You will become more confident and relaxed about the exciting possibilities of silkscreening.

GLUE STENCILS

10

In the GLUE method of stencilmaking, a diluted mixture of glue (usually LEPAGE'S GLUE) is applied to the screen. When it is dry it forms the stencil by blocking out the screen as desired. The glue acts on the same principle as the paper method, but the results are quite different from the big, open spaces, the clean knife-cut edges, or the torn edges of paper stencils.

With the glue method you can get drips, spatters, crumbly edges, and broken tones, in short, a more painterly effect. This is because your stencil is a liquid

Figure 10.1 With the glue method, very painterly effects, such as drips and spatters, can be achieved.

and is applied to the screen with all the flexibility, versatility, and fluidity of paint. If you want to print a big, open space it would be easier and quicker to use the paper-stencil method; using the glue method for effects that can be achieved more easily with another method would be pointless.

Basically, in the glue method, the screen is blocked out with glue wherever you do not want to print. **Where there is glue the ink will not go through.** The reason that this works is quite simple: the glue is water-soluble and the ink is oil base. Water and oil don't mix. When you print with oil-base inks, neither the action of the squeegee nor the cleanup with paint thinner will disturb or deteriorate the stencil. When you finally want to remove a glue stencil, simply wash the screen under warm water until it no longer feels slimy. Of course, after you have finished printing, the ink is the first thing that should be cleaned off.

The Lepage's glue should be thinned with water to make it a good consistency for painting—usually about $\frac{1}{3}$ water to $\frac{2}{3}$ glue is a good ratio. It can be stored in a jar indefinitely. [A ready-to-use glue solution called BLOCK-OUT can be bought at silkscreen suppliers.] You will find it helpful to add a little food coloring or India ink to the glue mixture to make the glue stencil more visible, since the glue by itself is colorless.

To begin, apply the glue to the screen to form a stencil. Paint it on the side of the screen facing you. You can position a drawing or sketch underneath the screen and use it as a guide. Or you can trace your design on the screen itself with a soft, leaded pencil.

Brushes of all sizes and kinds can be used to apply the glue, and your technique does not always have to be straightforward or involve just very simple shapes. You can play around with the glue and experiment to find out all the crazy, exciting things you can do: as with paint, you can drip it, smudge it on, splatter it, stamp it on, use it with a sponge—in other words, there is really no limit to the possible variety of effects.

Figure 10.2 A stencil is being painted on the screen with a diluted mixture of Lepage's glue. A sketch underneath the screen serves as a guide.

As you are applying the glue, keep your screen raised up slightly off the baseboard so that the glue will not leak through to the baseboard, and be sure the glue is dry before you start to print. Using a hair dryer will save a lot of time. Just be careful that the hair dryer does not touch the silk itself, since dryers sometimes become hot enough to burn a hole in your screen.

Because the glue is not affected by the ink or thinner, it will remain intact on your screen. Therefore, it is possible to add more glue to an already existing stencil. You can build up a print by adding new glue shapes to your screen with each successive printing. For example, you could start by printing a few glue shapes in a light color. After the ink has been cleaned off the screen, you can add more glue to the original stencil and overprint what you previously printed in a darker color, and so forth. You can keep on adding glue to produce as many additional colors as you want. Just be sure that there is sufficient contrast between the colors so they will be noticeable. This method makes for very easy registration because you are working from the same exact stencil for all the colors—you do not have to think about TRAPS and overlaps.

This **progressive glue method** (as I like to call it) is similar to the practice in block printing in which you start off by printing the whole block first, then gouge out some of the block and overprint, then gouge out more of the same block and again overprint, and so on.

Figure 10.3 A hair dryer can be used to dry glue and film stencils quickly. Be sure to keep the dryer at least 3″ from the silk.

Figure 10.4 Tusche, a liquid resist, is applied very thickly to the screen with a brush.

You should be aware that the areas to which the glue is applied do **not** print; this is almost like working in reverse. It can sometimes be frustrating and very difficult to visualize. Also glue stencils can prove time consuming if you have open lines and small details that you want to print. To do such a design and work more directly, you can use the resist method, in which the design is applied directly to the screen just as you want it to print.

A resist is simply something that resists or repels the glue. Substances that are very oily or greasy will not mix with or disturb water-soluble glue. The resist most often used is TUSCHE (pronounced "toosh"). This is a liquid, much like India ink but very oily and greasy. A design painted directly on the screen with tusche will repel the glue when dry. Tusche also comes in stick form. It resembles charcoal but is quite greasy. Stick tusche can be used to produce shadings and broken tones. Rubbings can be made directly on the screen from things that have interesting textures. Other substances that can be used as resists are crayons, oil crayons (Cray-pas), lipstick, and so forth.

Figure 10.5 Rubbings can be done directly on the screen with crayons, stick tusche, or oil pastels.

Whatever resist you are using, be absolutely certain that it is applied to the screen sufficiently—this means thick enough to fill the mesh of the silk. If you are using liquid tusche, you may have to apply more than one coat. If you are using crayons, really rub them in. Resists are never harmful to the silk, so apply them thickly enough to repel the glue. The way to check that the resist has been applied properly is to hold the screen up to a source of light and make sure there are no pinholes. Applying a resist is what gives most beginners problems in the glue stencil method. You will probably have to exaggerate your design somewhat, and you should avoid those designs with extremely fine lines or very clean-cut geometric shapes. These effects can be easily achieved with less frustration by using the film method described in Chapters 11 and 12.

Assuming that you have applied the tusche properly, let it dry thoroughly (again, a hair dryer is helpful here) and then go on to the next step—applying the glue. Remember that the resists themselves can never be used as a stencil because they are oil base and the ink will dissolve them. It is the glue that will form your stencil.

The glue will be applied over the total area of the screen. It will go over the resist but will not stick to it. Apply two thorough but thin coats of the diluted Lepage's glue. Don't bother using a brush for this.

Figures 10.6 and 10.7 Two prints made from original drawings done directly on the screen by 9-year-old children. Crayon was the resist for the glue.

Simply pour about a half-ounce of the glue onto the screen. Use a small square of rigid cardboard, and squeegee the glue back and forth and up and down over the entire area of your screen. Then scrape the excess glue back into the jar.

Let the screen dry for about ten minutes and apply a second coat in the same manner. It is very risky to try to get away with only one coat. There might be some bubbles in the first coat or you might have missed a few spots, which will result in a leaky stencil.

After the second coat of glue is dry, the resist must be dissolved from the screen. Place your screen on newspaper, pour on some paint thinner, and use a rag or an old toothbrush to remove the resist, just as you do to clean ink from your screen. If the resist has been applied thickly enough, the thinner will dissolve it in a matter of minutes. And, wherever you applied the resist, you will have an open area on your screen. Of

Figure 10.8 Glue is poured on the screen, completely covering the resist. A cardboard square is used to squeegee the glue as close to the silk as possible.

Figure 10.9 The resist is dissolved from the screen with paint thinner. A toothbrush can help dissolve it faster.

course, if the resist was not thick enough it will not completely wash out, and your design will be incomplete or will lack some important lines.

After you have dissolved the resist, wipe the thinner off the screen with rags, align your register corner correctly with your paper, and proceed to print.

To remove your stencil, take the pins out of the hinges and carry only the screen to the sink.

It's comforting to know that no matter how long a glue stencil has been left on your screen, it can always be removed simply by washing the screen with warm water.

Be sure that you are always using Lepage's glue or a similar glue that remains water-soluble when dry. Stay

Figure 10.10 Warm water dissolves the glue from the screen. When the screen no longer feels slimy, it is clean.

away from products, such as Elmer's Glue, which form an insoluble plastic when they are dry and cannot be removed from the silk.

Another type of liquid stencil can be made by brushing lacquer or nail polish on the silk. Since this type of stencil is not affected by water or oil, it can be used both with water-soluble inks such as Prang Textile Inks and with oil-base inks. Lacquer stencils can be dissolved with lacquer thinner or nail polish remover.

Experience will allow you to do these methods well as you get the feel of working with the glue and resists. You will also see that this method, like all such creative activities, is well suited to a very personal kind of expression as the stencil is formed.

THE HAND-CUT FILM METHOD

11

This is the method to use when you have a design that has a lot of small, loose floating parts or a variety of shapes which must have clean, very precise corners and edges. FILM stencils are also called for when you have a design that you want to keep on the screen for reprinting after cleanup. A paper stencil must be removed when the screen is cleaned and cannot be reused. Also, this method is impractical for a design with many small, loose floating parts. The cut film method, with its plastic backing sheet that holds all these parts together until the film has been attached securely to the screen, makes it easy to do this type of design. Although you can use the glue method, your components will appear to have a painted edge. If you want clean edges and angles, knife-cut film is best.

Figure 11.1 A knife-cut film stencil allows for more intricate designs than those possible with paper stencils.

The film originally designed for use in commercial silkscreening to achieve a durable, clean-edged stencil comes in the form of a laminated, transparent sheet. There are two different types of film: **lacquer film** and **water-soluble film.** Both are structured in the same way. They have a clear base layer of plastic and, on top of that, a film of flexible lacquer or glue. This top layer, which is tinted to make it easily distinguishable from the plastic base, will form the stencil on the silk. The areas to be printed (the open areas) are formed on the film by first cutting them with a sharp knife and then peeling them off the film. The film is then adhered to the mesh of the screen using water or, in the case of LACQUER FILM, lacquer thinner. When the film has dried, the plastic backing sheet is peeled off, leaving the green film attached to the silk. The film, of course, blocks out the ink just as paper and glue do. It can be removed after the ink is cleaned off by using the appropriate solvent, either water or lacquer thinner.

Examples of the two types of film are ULANOCUT GREEN (water-soluble) and STASHARP (lacquer film). Both types are structured and operate in the same way. The difference lies in the way each adheres to and is removed from the screen. The lacquer film, the first to be developed, consists of a layer of lacquer lightly bonded to a sheet of transparent plastic. After lacquer film has been cut and peeled, it is affixed to the silk by using a special film-adhering liquid or lacquer thinner.

It can be removed by dissolving it with a greater amount of lacquer thinner.

Water-soluble films are a more recent development; Ulanocut Green, for example, has been designed to adhere to the screen with plain water. Older types of water-soluble film required using a mixture of vinegar and alcohol as an adhering liquid. Water-soluble films are removed by thoroughly rinsing them in water, exactly as you would to remove a glue stencil.

Both types of film produce the same results and are cut in the same way. Some fabric inks, such as **Prang Textile** inks, contain water and oil mixed together in an emulsion. If they are used with a water-soluble stencil, the stencil will start to dissolve and deteriorate. For printing with oil-base poster inks, however, water-soluble films have definite advantages in the long run. There is no need to use lacquer thinner with its extremely strong fumes. Then, too, it is certainly easier to remove a stencil with water. The films will store easily if they are kept from extremes of temperature and humidity. A cardboard tube makes an ideal container to prevent wrinkling and absorption of dust.

Both lacquer and water-soluble films are usually the same transparent green color. If you are not sure which type of film you have, you can try sticking a wet finger on the film side. If the finger sticks, the film is water-soluble. If not, it is the lacquer type.

There are three steps in using the film: **cutting, peeling,** and **adhering.**

To cut the film, place the green or tinted side of the film faceup on top of the layout. The plastic side should rest on the layout. The piece of film should have a border about $\frac{3}{4}''$ bigger than the layout, but it does not have to cover the entire screen. It will be both quicker and cheaper to block out the rest of the screen with strips of tracing paper and tape. Do not use a piece of film that is too big for the screen. Try to use a size that will leave a little margin of silk around it because the film will not stick to the shellacked edges of your taped border. Tape can be used to seal the film to the edge of the screen when you are ready to print.

Figure 11.2 A piece of Ulanocut Green is positioned on top of a layout, ready to be cut.

Always cut the film on a smooth, flat surface. The baseboard of the screen is ideal for this. First tape the film lightly to the baseboard, as you did with the paper stencil, keeping the layout underneath. Using a sharp knife, trace on the film layer only the areas of your design that are to be printed. If your layout involves more than one color, you will need a separate piece of film for each color unless you are planning to overlap transparent colors to produce new shades. If you have fairly well-separated areas of color, you can block one color with tracing paper while printing the other color. If you have butt registration, pay careful attention to cutting the TRAPS. It will be much more accurate to cut the stencils as you have printed them. Then you will know exactly where the previous colors are, as in the paper stencil method.

Figure 11.3 The green layer of the film is being cut with an X-acto knife, using a sharp blade and a light touch. The areas to be printed are peeled out of the film.

After you have traced the areas that are to be printed, lift up the edges of these shapes with the tip of your knife or a pair of tweezers and remove the film from the backing sheet. These will be open areas on the screen, or printed spaces, once the film has adhered and the backing sheet has been peeled off. If you have been using a sharp blade, these areas should come out smoothly and cleanly with no ragged edges. If you make a mistake in cutting the film, simply redraw the line and peel accordingly. Merely cutting the film will not cause it to print. You have to actually remove the film layer. Thus clean, precise angles and corners can be achieved by extending the lines forming each shape and peeling only the shape. The cuts of the knife that extend beyond the shape will weld together when the film is adhered to the silk.

Figure 11.4 A piece of hand-cut film illustrating how lines cut with a knife are extended to form clean-angled shapes.

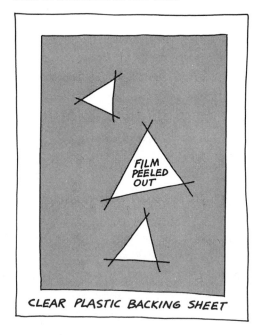

FILM PEELED OUT

CLEAR PLASTIC BACKING SHEET

With practice, almost any kind of layout can be cut using an X-acto knife with a sharp blade. There are, of course, special film-cutting tools available for cutting perfect arcs, circles, and parallel lines, but they are quite expensive. More practice with the X-acto knife will do the trick as well as save you money. There are also swivel knives with a rotating blade that are good for designs involving many curves. Film line cutters, available in three widths, have a loop of sharp steel at one end. They will cut and peel thin lines on the film, but they do not work well on small, intricate curves or lettering.

When you are cutting film, be sure to use a sharp blade and a light touch. Have refill blades or a small, fine-grained sharpening stone at hand. **It is important to cut the film layer only and not disturb the plastic backing sheet.** If you use too much pressure when

Figure 11.5 Film line cutters cut and peel thin lines in the film.

cutting the film, the backing sheet will become bumpy and warped instead of remaining flat. This will present problems when film is being adhered. Small puddles of water or lacquer thinner will form in the depressions of the plastic. The clear edges of the design will dissolve, giving the impression of burnt edges, and the stencil will not be strong. You should practice cutting and adhering small pieces of film until you have gotten the feel of doing it and can do it with confidence. And, relax! As you cut each piece, turn the film over and feel the plastic backing sheet. If you can feel where you have cut with the knife, then you are using too much pressure. Remember that the backing sheet should feel perfectly flat after the film has been cut and peeled.

The film must be securely adhered to the screen in order to form the stencil. Place the cut, peeled piece of film, film side up, on a BUILD-UP BOARD. This is a piece of flat, thick cardboard slightly smaller than the inside dimensions of your screen. Its purpose is to bring the silk and the film into as close contact as possible.

You can adhere a film stencil anywhere that seems convenient on the screen; simply adjust the register corner when you are ready to print. I mention this because it is very difficult to adhere the film in a precise spot when it is on a build-up board.

The film is bonded to the screen by dissolving a small portion of the film layer through the silk. This makes it sticky and lets it grip onto the mesh of the silk.

Figure 11.6 The piece of film is placed on a build-up board so that good contact with the silk will be established.

Lower the screen onto the film. If you are using a water-soluble film such as Ulanocut Green, you will use water as an adhering fluid. If you have lacquer film such as Stasharp, then use either the special adhering fluid sold for this film or lacquer thinner.

It is very important that nylon and other synthetic screen fabrics be treated with a slight abrasive in order to make the water-soluble films adhere well. Ajax cleanser, Ulano Microgrit, or silicon carbide 500 grit are some of the things you can use. Among these, however, Ajax or a similar cleanser is cheapest and easiest to find.

Sprinkle some Ajax on the stencil side of a wet screen. Use your hand to rub it over the entire area of the screen until it disappears to the other side. Repeat this about two or three more times. When you have completed this roughing up, be sure to rinse the screen thoroughly to remove all the particles of cleanser or they will clog the screen.

This treatment is necessary to give synthetic fabrics a "tooth" so they will grip onto film stencils. Natural silk requires no such treatment because it is a polyfilament whose fibers are already fuzzy and rough. Synthetic

Figure 11.7 An abrasive, such as Ajax cleanser, is used to prepare synthetic screens for water-soluble films. Be sure to rinse the abrasive thoroughly from the screen.

fibers are usually monofilaments with slick, smooth fibers. Treating them with an abrasive grit merely makes them more like natural fibers.

You are now ready to adhere the film. Use a small absorbent rag and apply water or lacquer thinner to a small area of the film. The rag should be wet but not sopping. The film needs only to be moistened with the appropriate fluid. Do not rub the film. When the film turns a darker shade, that means it has been moistened enough. Try to work quickly in an even pattern from one side of the screen to the other. Do small areas at a time. This way you will avoid air bubbles. It is easier to adhere water-soluble film to the silk if the screen has been premoistened with water before it is brought down on the film. The silk will then be more receptive to the film.

After you have adhered the film, blot the screen with a clean, dry rag. This will remove any excess fluid and help speed up the drying.

If the film has been correctly cut, with the backing sheet remaining flat, it should have good contact with the silk and the adhering will be quick and easy. However, if it has been cut too deeply, the contact, even with a build-up board, will be bad. This will show

Figure 11.8 The film is being adhered to the screen with a wet rag.

up as spots that do not darken as the film is adhered, and water or lacquer thinner is likely to form puddles and destroy any sharp edges. Parts of the stencil will tend to dissolve and others will peel off with the backing sheet.

Figure 11.9 The film is blotted gently with a dry rag.

The moral here is that the proof lies in a well-cut film. **Get in the good habit of using a sharp knife and a light touch.** It is worth repeating this because most of the problems with cut film are related to the actual cutting.

Now that the difficult tasks have been accomplished, let the film dry completely. A hair dryer or a fan can be expedient here. When the film is dry, it should not feel cool to the touch and will usually become lighter in color. Be sure that the film is completely dry before you try to peel off the backing sheet; otherwise you will unwittingly remove some the stencil. Use a fingernail to lift the backing sheet, which should now come off cleanly. Then, once you adjust the register corner according to your layout and block out the open areas of the screen around the piece of film with tape or tracing paper, you are ready to print your stencil.

A film stencil is quite durable. It will suffer no damage if you leave it on while you clean the screen with paint thinner, and it will remain undisturbed by printing. The film can also safely stay on the screen without harm to the screen fabric. It is possible to print the same stencil in different colors or to mask out parts of the stencil and overprint with other colors.

Figure 11.10 After the
film has dried, the plastic
backing is peeled off.

A water-soluble film is removed from the screen by
washing out with water—just as you would remove a
glue stencil. Run the screen under warm water until it
no longer feels slimy to the touch. You can actually see
the stencil dissolve.

A lacquer film stencil is removed by dissolving it with
lacquer thinner. Place the screen on top of old
newspapers and soak it with lacquer thinner. As the
stencil dissolves, change the newspaper and repeat the

Figure 11.11 Strips of paper can be used to block out large areas around the design. The piece of film should be slightly larger than the design, but it does not have to cover the whole screen.

application of lacquer thinner until the screen is completely clean. Try to avoid getting the lacquer thinner onto the shellacked border, as this solvent sometimes softens and partially dissolves shellac.

Cut-film stencils are well suited for printing greeting cards, which can be used year-round. Many people prefer sending a card to a friend rather than a letter on a plain piece of white paper, and how wonderful if it's your very own design. The stencil can be kept on the screen indefinitely and it is also possible to cut small, intricate designs. Cards can be printed on paper thick enough to be folded and remain rigid. Cover stock such as Becket Cover is recommended for printing cards. It folds easily and is available in a range of ten colors. It is sold in large sheets in most art-supply stores and can be cut to your exact specifications upon purchase. You should buy your envelopes ahead of time and have the cover stock cut to fit them. A good rule to remember is that a folded card should be about $\frac{1}{4}''$ smaller than the dimensions of the envelope. Print the cards flat so that they will be easy to register. If you are printing a large batch of cards, it will be too time consuming to hang each one up on a line to dry. Instead you could lay them out on large sheets of heavy cardboard as they are printed, and move these cardboard trays to a convenient drying area. A good number of cards can fit on each cardboard and you will be able to print more quickly and efficiently.

Figure 11.12 Greeting cards can be positioned on large sheets of rigid cardboard and allowed to dry.

12

In the photo method, a stencil is formed by the process of exposing through a transparent positive onto a piece of special photo-stencil film. This film is then developed and adhered to the screen. With this method you can print photographic images, very fine lines and lettering, intricate details in drawings, and so forth. All of the seemingly complex things that could not be done with the other methods can be done precisely and easily with the photo method.

The photo method actually demands very little equipment. You will probably find that you already have many of the things you need. Most important, the film is easy to handle, and you do not need a darkroom to expose the film. The film used is a presensitized photo-stencil film. It is already sensitive to ultraviolet light. The film can be purchased in art-supply stores that sell silkscreen supplies under several different brand names, the most common being BLUE POLY 2 and HI-FI GREEN. Both of these are made by the Ulano Company. Stenciling with all of the presensitized films involves the same four basic steps: expose the film, develop it, wash it out, and then adhere it to the screen.

A sheet of the photo-stencil film resembles a sheet of colored transparent plastic or hand-cut film and, like the latter, is composed of two layers: a sheet of clear plastic and an emulsion layer (usually blue or green) which is light sensitive.

It is the glue-like emulsion which will form your stencil after it has been exposed and developed. The layer of plastic acts as a temporary support. It is removed before printing—after the film has been adhered to the screen and dried.

The film can be stored indefinitely in the black tube it is sold in. It should be kept away from ultraviolet light such as sun rays and fluorescent light. However, it can be removed from its tube and cut under incandescent light, which is the light from a regular round light bulb, with no danger of deterioration from fogging. During the actual exposure, you do not have to worry about daylight or other light harming it. It is pretty easy to handle.

To produce the stencil on the film you have to expose through something called a **positive** onto the film. It is essentially like making a contact print. In very simple terms, a POSITIVE is a thin, flat sheet composed of clear and opaque areas. This allows the light to penetrate to the film or be blocked from it as you desire. A positive is used like a negative, but it must contain no shaded areas and must be the same size as your finished stencil.

There are many different kinds of positives. You can make your own with pen and ink, you can make (or have made) photographic positives, or you can use string, pieces of lace, or other flat objects.

Figure 12.1 Some of the material that can be used to produce positives on acetate.

Figure 12.2 A piece of macramé placed on a piece of the photo-stencil film acts as a positive. The screen will print wherever the light is blocked out.

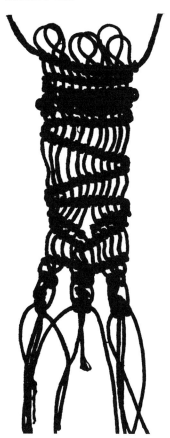

You can use ink on ACETATE to do very fine drawings and small lettering and calligraphy. You then expose through this onto the film to produce your stencil. The open areas of your stencil will correspond exactly to those shapes and lines on the acetate covered by black opaque ink, that is, those areas where the light does not get to the film. Just be sure that the black lines on your positive *are* black and opaque. If they are not, they will not become adequately etched on your stencil film.

Acetate has a different surface from paper. Regular India ink does not work well on it. Be sure to use a special acetate ink with your pens. Higgin's Black Magic ink is recommended. Also try to keep the acetate clean and free from grease, which will make it difficult to draw on.

Working on acetate allows a lot more flexibility than working on paper. You can easily overlap pieces and cut or scrape away mistakes. You can do words, designs, and so forth on strips of acetate, cut them up,

Figure 12.3 A photo stencil produced from an ink drawing on acetate allows thin lines to be printed clearly, as in this card handscreened by Martha Friedman, 1976.

Figure 12.4 Words done on acetate strips and other flat, opaque materials can be manipulated until a satisfying layout is achieved.

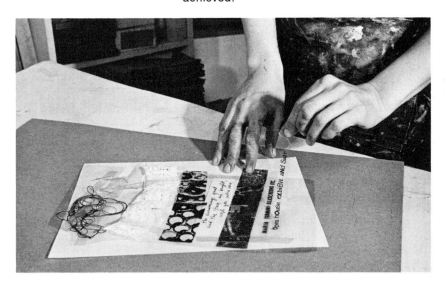

and play around with various combinations until you have them the way you want. Then, you can scotch tape them to another piece of acetate. The pieces of scotch tape will not show when you expose the film because they are transparent.

If you want to use a certain kind of type for lettering, you can do this easily by using a commercial art product known as transfer type, which comes in large sheets of letters according to the kind and size of type you want. To use transfer type, position the particular letter on top of a piece of acetate and rub it with a ballpoint pen. The letter transferred to the acetate is opaque and will work perfectly to block out the light when the film is exposed. Wherever you have a black letter, you will have an open area on your screen. This is where the ink goes through, and this is what will print.

Transfer type is very useful when you are designing posters or business cards. It produces a neat, precise kind of type. Letraset and Chart-Pak are two brand names of transfer type. You should be sure that the sheets you buy are fresh. If they are old, they will not transfer neatly.

If you want to make silkscreen prints of photographs, your photographs have to be converted into positives, clear and black, with no gray areas. This is usually

OK

MARIA
TERMINI

murals, banners,
special effects, and
silkscreen prints

OK

Figure 12.5 Transfer type was used to make a positive on acetate of a particular kind of lettering. Rubylith, a masking film, was used to make the positives for the shapes.

accomplished by making a HIGH-CONTRAST print from your negative on a special kind of film called KODALITH, which, as its name implies, is made by Kodak. This plastic-base, high-contrast film does not produce any shades of gray. You then expose through the Kodalith positive to the photo-stencil film.

Figure 12.6 A high-contrast print made from a 35 mm black-and-white negative.

Most photographs contain black and white plus many different shades of gray. Thus, although any negative can be made into a high-contrast positive by enlarging it onto a sheet of Kodalith, some detail will be lost. Some of the gray areas will drop out and become clear and others will become black. It follows that not all continuous-tone negatives will make good, intelligible high-contrast positives for silkscreening. Only those photographs that have a good amount of contrast to begin with will work as clear positives.

If you have access to a darkroom, you can make Kodalith positives yourself. More detailed technical information will be provided by the data sheet that comes with the box of film. If you do not have a darkroom or the spare time, however, you can have high-contrast positives made at a printer's or photo reproduction shop.

There is no one set correct exposure time for Kodalith. One exciting thing you can try is to make two or more different stencils by using that number of high-contrast positives produced at different exposure times. Each positive will have a different density and, therefore, a different configuration of the same image. Series of positives are known as **tone separations**, which can be printed over each other in a variety of color combinations. Effects such as this—getting a color print from a black and white negative—are why photo silkscreening cannot be labeled a cut-and-dried technique. There is always plenty of room for originality, imagination, and experimenting with unknown possibilities.

Photographs can also be converted into HALFTONES on acetate. In this process the image is translated into a configuration of tiny black dots, which actually

Figure 12.7 A halftone made from a 35 mm black-and-white negative.

eliminates the gray but retains the illusion of gray from the way that the dots are dispersed. You can have halftones made at the printer's. You can also make them yourself by using a special film called Autoscreen (by Kodak) and enlarging onto Kodalith in a darkroom.

Other easily obtainable positives include string, ferns, and pieces of lace, to list just a few. These are simply placed on top of the stencil film, which is exposed through them. Just be sure that what you use is opaque and will stay flat and make good contact with the film.

So we see that all kinds of things will work as positives as long as the image (that is, what you want to print) is opaque. Avoid having gray in the positive because it will appear as a filled-in area and will not print. You can also combine positives by placing them on top of each other when exposing the film. In addition, you can take ink and write words all over Kodalith positives. The variety is endless.

After you have made or found your positive, you are then ready to expose the film, the Blue Poly 2 or the Hi-Fi Green. In this step the film will be cut photochemically, just as hand-cut film is cut with a knife.

The least expensive setup for exposing the film is made with a no. 2 photo-flood bulb, available from any camera store. You will need a special holder because the bulb gets too hot for a regular socket.

Position the film 12″ from the light bulb so that it will not warp from the heat. The film should be exposed on a flat surface and placed emulsion-side down. If you are in doubt as to which side this is, touch a wet finger to the film—the sticky side is the emulsion, essentially glue. Remember, the film must always be exposed through the plastic side or it will not react photochemically to form your stencil.

Your positive is then placed on top of the film—**reversed.** This is essential, especially if you are using letters, or your stencil will come out backwards. Think of it as making a four-layer sandwich:

Figure 12.8

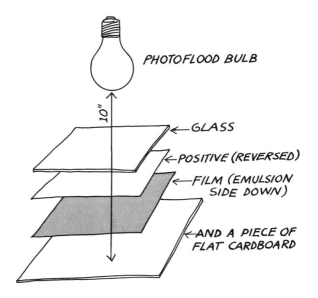

10″

PHOTOFLOOD BULB

←GLASS

←POSITIVE (REVERSED)

←FILM (EMULSION SIDE DOWN)

←AND A PIECE OF FLAT CARDBOARD

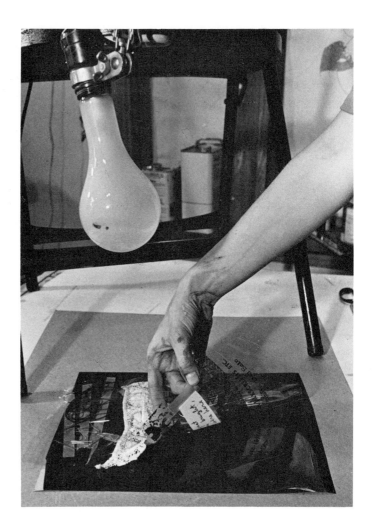

Figure 12.9 The various positives are placed, reversed, on a piece of photo-stencil film that has been placed emulsion side down on a flat surface.

The glass is used to hold everything flat and to ensure good contact between the film and the positive. The piece of film that you use need only extend about 1″ around your design. You can block out the rest of your screen later with paper or glue. Exposing the film for 10 minutes usually produces good results when using a no. 2 photo-flood lamp.

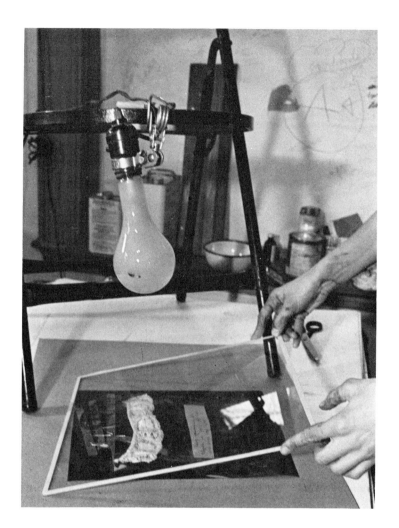

Figure 12.10 A piece of clean glass holds the film and the positive in close contact. The film is ready to be exposed using a simple setup with the photoflood lamp clamped onto a chair.

No matter what kind of positive you are using, exposure time will not be affected. If you are using a different light source, however—sunlight, a sunlamp, or a carbon arc lamp—you will need a different exposure time. To discover the correct exposure time, make a test strip: cover up the film with a piece of black paper at 1-minute intervals. After the film has been developed you should be able to tell how long an exposure you need to produce a healthy stencil.

Proper exposure time will make a difference in stencil quality. On a correctly exposed piece of film, the emulsion that remains should be the same color as it was before the film was exposed. If the film is underexposed, a lot of the emulsion will wash off and the film will appear lighter in color. Such a weak stencil will most likely leak. On the other hand, if the film is overexposed, the emulsion will look thicker and darker in color than normal. The danger here is that when the film is adhered to the screen some of the very small spaces and thin lines in your design will get filled in by the too-thick emulsion. The resulting print will not be nearly as precise or complete as your positive.

Immediately after the film has been exposed, place it emulsion-side up in the developer for $1\frac{1}{2}$ minutes. The areas exposed to the light will become hardened, and the unexposed areas will remain soft. These unexposed areas will later wash away. You can use the developer that comes with the film, which consists of two kinds of powder that you mix with water in certain quantities: A AND B DEVELOPER. You can also use a mixture of $\frac{1}{2}$ ten-volume HYDROGEN PEROXIDE (3%) and $\frac{1}{2}$ water. This is cheaper and easier, since you don't have to measure and dissolve powders. Also it lets you mix only what you need—just enough developer to cover the film.

Figure 12.11 The film is placed in the developer emulsion side up and rocked gently for $1\frac{1}{2}$ minutes.

The film can be developed in a special developing tray, a glass baking dish, or the vegetable bin from your refrigerator. Avoid using metal. As the film is being developed, rock the tray back and forth so that the developer flows over the film, and avoid rubbing it with your fingers. The emulsion is quite "gooey" and you will only ruin it or scratch it. At this stage you do not see your image but only a white scum forming on top of the film.

The same tray of developing solution can be used for several pieces of film, provided that you keep the tray covered after the first piece of film has been developed. This is necessary because some of the light-sensitive particles from the film get into the developer and will cause it to rot if exposed to the light. Do not try to keep the developer overnight or store it in a bottle after it has been used. Mix it fresh each day.

After developing, the film is washed out in hot running water until the image is clear. Support the film, emulsion-side up, on a piece of plastic or glass.

Figure 12.12 The film, supported on a piece of glass, is rinsed thoroughly in hot water until the image is clear.

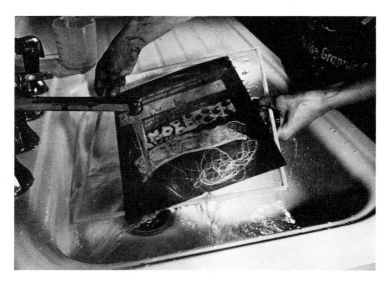

The water used to rinse the film should be quite hot, about as hot as your hands can stand it. The washing out is completed when all the places that were black on your positive (i.e., where the film was not exposed to light) are free of emulsion and completely clear. The piece of film now looks like a negative. There should be no shades of emulsion, no light blue or green. It should be one even color.

What you have at this stage is exactly what you have after you have cut and peeled a piece of hand-cut film. The big difference is that with the photo method the film is "cut" and removed photochemically. The emulsion remains supported by the plastic backing sheet, as in the hand-cut film method.

After the film has been washed clear by the hot water, rinse it in cold water for a few seconds to harden the emulsion a bit. Otherwise, when you adhere it to the screen, it will be so soft that you will blot too much of it away.

Be ready to adhere the film as soon as it has been washed out. Have a clean screen and a build-up board ready. Place the film (emulsion-side up) on the build-up board, then lower your screen on top of the film. Blot the film through the silk with single sheets of newspaper. Continue blotting until no more film or water comes through on the newspaper. It is normal that some of the emulsion will stain the newspaper as

Figure 12.13 The film is placed on a build-up board and is ready to be adhered to the silk.

Figure 12.14 The film is adhered by blotting it through the silk with pieces of newspaper.

you are blotting. This is the adhering process in the photo method; since the film is already wet, you don't need a special adhering solution. Merely blotting the film will cause it to stick to the screen by forcing the silk into the emulsion layer.

If you are using a nylon or polyester screen, you should rough up the back of your silk with a gritty cleanser so that it will be fuzzier and grip the stencil better. This has been described in Chapter 11.

You should also be sure that the screen is perfectly free of greasy traces of thinner or ink. Trisodium phosphate, a powdered cleaning agent available in hardware stores, is recommended for this.

Now let the film dry completely. Again, a hair dryer will expedite matters. If the stencil feels cool to the touch, it is still wet, and trying to peel off the backing sheet will remove parts of the stencil. When completely dry, the backing sheet will separate easily from the stencil.

After you have taped down your register corner and blocked out the rest of your screen, you are ready to print. Try to print your stencil with one quick stroke of the squeegee. If you go over it a number of times, the fine lines and small dots will get thick and fuzzy.

One other hint: if you are going to use glue to block out your screen, apply the glue right after you have blotted the film. That way, the stencil and the glue can dry at the same time.

Photo stencils are extremely durable. You can print and clean them as many times as you want and, if they have been properly adhered, they will not deteriorate. Eventually they can be removed from your screen with warm water and a special ENZYME SCREEN CLEANER. You can also substitute an enzyme presoak such as Axion, which is much cheaper and is available in any supermarket. Sprinkle some of the Axion on the back of the wet screen, rub it in, and then rinse out your stencil. (Of course, you should always completely remove all the ink first!)

The photo-stencil method I have explained in this chapter is known as the **indirect method** because the film is exposed separately from the screen and then adhered. I feel that this is the simplest method, because it can be done in normal room light and goes rather quickly. However, I should mention that there is another photo method known as the **direct method** in which the screen itself is coated with a sensitized emulsion and the positive is exposed directly onto the screen. This method is much more time consuming and inconvenient, since it requires working in a darkened room and considerable waiting while the coatings dry on the screen. Then, too, a direct stencil must be removed from your screen with bleach, so that only nylon (no silk) screens may be used. Taking all this into consideration, the indirect film method has a number of advantages over the direct method.

FABRIC PRINTING

13

Fabric printing is a practical application of silkscreening. Certainly one derives a sense of satisfaction and excitement from wearing clothes made from a self-designed fabric. Fabric can be used for scarves, draperies, bags, and wall coverings. Printing on tee shirts is a way of getting a message across in both designs and words. Many businesses are using tee shirts as a means of advertising.

The main difference between fabric printing and printing on paper is that in fabric printing the screen is used by itself detached from the baseboard. The screen is positioned on the fabric and moved around each time the design is to be repeated.

The fabric is stretched tightly on a flat surface. A smooth layer of newspapers underneath the fabric will provide the right amount of padding. If you are printing on tee shirts, put a large piece of cardboard inside the shirt to stretch it and to prevent the ink from smudging on the other side of the shirt.

A large table or even a smooth floor is a fine working surface. The fabric can be kept stretched out with masking tape or pushpins. It should be smooth and wrinkle-free.

Fabric has a more absorbent surface than paper and therefore requires special inks designed to penetrate deeper into the fabric fibers than regular poster-type inks. After the fabric has been printed with these inks, it is usually heat-set, with a hot iron or dryer, to make the colors as permanent as possible. It can then be washed without fading.

Prang and Nazdar are two of the brand names for fabric inks; each comes with its own specialized

Figure 13.1 Silkscreened banners hanging from my front porch.

Figure 13.2 A silkscreened skirt, bag, and shirt.

Figure 13.3 A paper stencil ready for printing on fabric. The fabric has been stretched wrinkle-free with masking tape over a smooth padding of newspapers.

instructions that should be available from your art supplier. Read these instructions carefully before you make your stencil. Some inks, such as Prang inks, are an emulsion of oil and water. This means that they cannot be used with a water-soluble stencil, such as photo-stencil film and glue stencils, as they will

Figure 13.4 Cardboard is used to stretch tee shirts flat and prevent the design from bleeding through to the other side.

dissolve the stencil. **Lacquer film** is the type of stencil that is recommended. If the ink is entirely oil base, however, such as the Nazdar textile inks, then glue and tracing-paper stencils can be used with no problem.

Fabric woven from natural fibers, especially cotton, is the easiest and most ink-receptive material to print on. Synthetic fibers such as Dacron and nylon are more difficult to print on because they are slicker and not as fuzzy or absorbent as natural fibers. Special inks have been formulated for these synthetic fibers.

Pure cotton sheets, cotton tee shirts, and muslin are examples of natural-fiber fabrics that can be easily printed with the inks that are more readily available. Before you print, newly purchased fabric should be washed to remove the sizing, a starch-like substance that acts as a barrier between the ink and the fibers. If the sizing remains on the fabric while it is being printed, the colors of your design will eventually fade. If you want a light-colored background, the fabric can be pretinted with a dye such as Rit.

Fabric inks are usually transparent. Be sure that you print your design with a color that is darker than the background. For example, an orange printed over a medium red would not be very noticeable. There are also rubber-base fabric inks that are completely opaque if you wish, for example, to print white letters on a black background or light colors over any darker background.

Before you start to print on fabric, it is a good idea to test-print the stencil on scrap paper to make sure that everything will be okay. Once fabric is printed, the design cannot be removed and another design overprinted. Make sure that there are no clogged areas in the silk that would produce a bad-quality print.

Also if you practice on scraps of fabric, you will get a good idea of just how much squeegee pressure is needed. Fabric has a greater absorbency than paper, so more ink has to go through the mesh of the silk. Using more squeegee strokes, a wider mesh of silk, and/or a rounded squeegee blade are ways to accomplish this.

Figure 13.5 As the fabric is printed, the screen is moved to repeat the design. One hand holds the screen steady while the other hand pulls the squeegee.

Start printing on a corner of the fabric. Remember how many squeegee strokes you have used, and try to use the same number of strokes each time the stencil is printed; otherwise there will be shade variations along the length of the fabric.

Be very careful not to let the screen shift around as you print. This will result in a smudgy design with sloppy edges. Learn to hold the screen steady or have an assistant hold the screen firmly in position while you squeegee. With some practice, you will be able to use squeegees of up to 12″ long with one hand. If you are printing on the floor with a large squeegee that requires both hands, the screen can be held steady with your foot.

Simple fabric designs can be printed by sight—that is, it is easy to see where the design is to repeat without a lot of measuring and marking off. If a block-type design, one that uses almost the entire area of the screen, is being printed, you should overlap the printed areas a little bit so that the design flows continuously with no background spaces between units.

More-complicated designs and those with more than one color require some system for correctly positioning the printing frame as you print. One method is to measure off the fabric before printing with colored thread or chalk into rectangles the size of the printing frame. These serve as guides for placing the screen on the fabric.

After the fabric has been printed, it should be allowed to dry thoroughly. This usually takes about three days. Most inks require that the fabric be heat-set in order to make the colors more permanent. Heat opens up the fibers so the dye can really penetrate. Ironing the fabric with a hot iron or putting it in a hot dryer for half an hour are simple ways to do this. Check the instructions for the particular brand of ink you are using. Once the colors have set, the fabric can be used or sewn into clothes that can be washed with no fear that the design will fade or run.

I hope I have given you a clear understanding of how the various stencil methods work—and some insight into the functional and enjoyable part silkscreening can play in your life. The more you print, the more exciting possibilities and projects will suggest themselves. Be open to alternatives. Colors do not always have to be laid down as planned. Try feeding the paper into the corner upside down just to see what happens, or overlap images from unrelated designs.

I consider silkscreening similar to the process of learning to play a musical instrument. Practice and organization will give you confidence and skill so you can improvise, enjoy, invent, and let the magic shine through.

APPENDIXES

A VISUAL EFFECTS
OF STENCIL METHODS

PAPER STENCILS

large, flat areas of color

clean or torn edges

not too many loose floating parts

GLUE STENCILS

thick lines

brushed shapes

rough edges

textures

shading

lettering—but not very small or with really thin lines

HAND-CUT FILM

lots of small floating parts

clean edges on geometric shapes

precise angles

PHOTO-STENCIL FILM

photographic images—those taken by a camera

half-tones and high contrast images

very fine lettering and calligraphy

ink drawings on acetate

PHOTO-STENCIL FILM
(continued)

transfer type on acetate

patterns from thin, flat, opaque objects such as string and lace

B MANUFACTURERS OF SILKSCREEN PRODUCTS

INKS

Serascreen Corporation
5-25 Forty-Seventh Road
Long Island City, N.Y. 11101

Naz-Dar
1087 North Branch St.
Chicago, Illinois 60622

Speedball Inks
Hunt Manufacturing Co.
1405 Locust St.
Philadelphia, Pa. 19109

Prang Textile Inks
American Crayon
Wayne and Monmouth Sts.
Jersey City, N.J. 07313

Kan-doc Inks
Kudner and O'Connor
4035 West Kinzie
Chicago, Illinois 60624

FILMS

Ulano Company, Inc.
610 Dean Street
Brooklyn, N.Y. 11238

C WHAT DISSOLVES WHAT

WATER	glue
	water-soluble blockout
	water-soluble film
	Ulanocut Green
	photo-stencil film
PAINT THINNER or	printing ink
TURPENTINE or	tusche
SCREENWASH or	crayons
KEROSENE or	oil pastels
MINERAL SPIRITS	
BRUSH CLEANER	dried ink
(not detergent type)	dried shellac
such as *Sterling*	
or *Kwik-eez*	
LACQUER THINNER or	lacquer film
ACETONE or	dried ink
NAIL POLISH REMOVER	nail polish
DENATURED ALCOHOL	wet shellac

GLOSSARY

A AND B DEVELOPER   two separately packaged powders
used to develop the photo-stencil film
manufactured by the Ulano Company.

ACETATE   sheets of clear plastic used with opaque ink
or transfer type to produce a positive image that
can be placed on photo-stencil film and exposed.

BLOCK OUT   to fill in the mesh of the silk in those areas
that are to remain unprinted; also glue which
forms the stencil.

BLUE POLY 2 OR 3   types of presensitized photo-stencil
film made by the Ulano Company.

BRUSH CLEANER   a strong solvent used for dissolving
dried ink from a screen, such as Sterling or Kwik-
eez; available in most hardware stores.

BUILD-UP BOARD   a piece of thick cardboard smaller than
the inside dimensions of the screen, used when
adhering film to the silk to bring about better
contact between the two elements.

BUTT REGISTRATION   a layout in which the various colors
are juxtaposed so as to eliminate white spaces
between them.

EDITION   the total number of prints of a particular
design or subject. The edition number is the
bottom half of the fraction on the lower left-hand
side of the print. The first part of the fraction is
the number of the print: 23/29 means that the
print is the 23rd print out of a total of 29.

EMULSION   the tinted layer on the photo-stencil film
which is adhered to the silk and forms the stencil.

ENZYME   screen-cleaner chemicals, such as Axion, used
to completely dissolve photo-stencils.

FILM   a laminated stencil that is cut either by hand or photographically and then adhered to the screen. A plastic backing sheet is used to support the film until it is adhered and dried on the screen, at which time it is peeled off leaving only the stencil material on the screen.

FLOATING PARTS   parts that are not connected to the body of the stencil, also known as **island parts.**

GLUE   a liquid, water-soluble stencil material, most often Lepage's glue.

GUMMED PAPER TAPE   tape that sticks by moistening it with water; used to seal the edges of the silk to the wood frame to prevent leakage of the ink.

HALFTONE   an interpretation of a continuous tone photograph into arrangements of minute black dots so that it can be printed with one color of ink.

HIGH-CONTRAST POSITIVE   a photograph composed solely of black and white elements. A high-contrast print on acetate is used to produce the stencil on photo-stencil film.

HI-FI GREEN   a type of presensitized photo-stencil film made by the Ulano Company.

HINGE BAR   a strip of wood the same thickness as the screen frame to which the frame is hinged if the baseboard is not thick enough to take screws.

HYDROGEN PEROXIDE   Can be used to develop the photo-stencil film.

KODALITH   a high-contrast film on an acetate base used to produce positives for photo-silkscreening.

LACQUER FILM   a hand-cut stencil film in which the stencil layer is a thin film of lacquer, usually green-colored.

LAYOUT   the plan of a projected print used as a guide for forming stencils and registering colors.

LEPAGE'S GLUE   a water-soluble glue used to form a stencil directly on the silk.

MESH   the tightness of the weave of a screen fabric. The lower the number, the wider the mesh; for example, 22 would be a very close-woven mesh.

MINERAL SPIRITS, PAINT THINNER   Used for cleaning the ink from the screen and for removing resists such as tusche or crayons.

POSITIVE   the artwork, halftone, or high-contrast print on acetate.

REGISTER CORNER   the position marked on the baseboard for placing printing paper in the same spot.

REGISTRATION   the process of aligning the various colors in a print.

SCREEN SUPPORT   a small piece of wood that automatically drops down from the screen frame as it is lifted.

SCREEN WASH   a solvent for cleaning the ink from the screen.

SERACRON   a brand of synthetic silk made from nylon.

SERIGRAPHY   another term for silkscreening; specifically, a serigraph is a fine-arts type of print as opposed to one produced for commercial purposes.

SHELLAC   used to waterproof and seal the gummed paper tape to the silk and frame.

SILK   the fabric that is stretched very tightly to the screen frame upon which the stencil is formed. Stencil silk is especially woven for the silkscreen process. Both natural and synthetic types are available.

SQUEEGEE   a thick blade of rubber in a wooden handle used to squeeze the ink through the mesh of the silk.

STASHARP   a brand of hand-cut film made by the Ulano Company.

STENCIL   that which blocks out the portions of the screen that are to remain unprinted.

TRACING PAPER   thin transparent paper used in making paper stencils.

TRANSFER TYPE   a commercial art product, such as Letraset, available in sheets of many different kinds and sizes of type. It can be transferred to sheets of acetate by rubbing the letters with a ballpoint pen. In this way, positives for photo-silkscreening can be produced.

TRANSPARENT BASE   a clear gel used to thin the ink to good consistency for printing and to make transparent colors from opaque ones.

TRAPS   underlaps and overlaps of color.

TURPENTINE   a chemical used to clean oil-base inks from the screen.

TUSCHE   a greasy ink used as a resist with glue stencils.

ULANOCUT GREEN   a water-soluble hand-cut stencil film made by the Ulano Company.

UNDERLAPS   places where the lighter colors are cut and printed a bit larger than they actually are to insure more perfect registration when the darker colors are printed over them.

WAX PAPER   used as a stencil material and to block out large areas of the screen.

X-ACTO KNIFE   a lightweight knife with a replaceable blade (no. 11 type blade) and a long handle used for cutting film and paper stencils.

INDEX

Enzyme screen cleaner, 153

F

Film stencils, 115, 162
   adhering, 122–25
   cutting, 118
   cutting tools, 121
   drying, 127
   lacquer base, 116, 123, 161
   manufacturer, 169
   removing, 128
   water-soluble, 116
Floating parts, 3, 13, 87, 115
Friedman, Martha, 136

G

"Garden in the Sky," Maria
   Termini (*see* color insert)
Goop, 64
"Go Slo," Corita Kent (*see* color
   insert)
Glue stencils, 101, 162
   drying, 104
   progressive glue stencils, 104
   removing, 111
Gummed paper tape, 32, 39
Gwathmy, Robert, 13

H

Halftones, 140, 142
Hamill, Tim, "Modular
   Pholage" (*see* color
   insert)
   "Negative Foliage" (*see*
   color insert)
   "Paleontologist's Dream"
   (*see* color insert)
Hand cleaner, 64
Hand-cut film (*see* film)

Heat setting, 16, 158, 164
Hicken, Philip, 13
Hi-Fi Green, 133
Higgins Black Magic Ink, 135
High-contrast positives, 74, 138,
   139
Hinge bar, 45
"Hot Guitar," Maria Termini
   (*see* color insert)
Hydrogen peroxide, 146

I

Indirect photo method (*see*
   Photo-stencil film)
Inks, 48
   fabric 57, 117, 157, 161
   manufacturers, 169
   rubber base, 161
   storing, 56
   water-soluble, 57
Island parts (*see* Floating parts)

K

Kent, Corita, 15
   "Go Slo" (*see* color insert)
   "The Legs of the Earth are
   My Legs" (*see* color
   insert)
King, Wendy, "Wendy's
   Garden" (*see* color insert)
Kodalith, 138, 140

L

Lacquer, 112
Lacquer film (*see* film)
Lacquer thinner, 116
Latos-Valier, Paula, "A Little
   Dab'll Do Ya" (*see* color
   insert)